A Tiny Step Away
from Deepest Faith

A Tiny Step Away from Deepest Faith

A TEENAGER'S SEARCH FOR MEANING

. . . . Marjorie
Corbman

PARACLETE PRESS
BREWSTER, MASSACHUSETTS

10 9 8 7 6 5 4 3 2 1

© 2005 by Marjorie Corbman
ISBN 1-55725-429-X

Library of Congress Cataloging-in-Publication Data
Corbman, Marjorie.
A tiny step away from deepest faith : a teenager's search for meaning /
by Marjorie Corbman.
       p.cm.
ISBN 1-55725-429-X
1. Corbman, Marjorie. 2. Orthodox Eastern converts—Biography.
3. Christian life—Orthodox Eastern authors. 4. Teenagers—Religious
life. I. Title.
BX395.C67A3 2005   248.2'46'092—dc22

Published by Paraclete Press
Brewster, Massachusetts
www.paracletepress.com

Printed in the United States of America.

For the family God has given me

—actual and adopted—

my parents, my sisters, and those friends who have become indelibly part of my life—

because, as Christine assures me, "that's what really matters,"

and especially for Kirsten and Rachel,

without whom I can't say what would have become of me.

Table of Contents

Foreword   ix

Introduction   1

ONE   9
How God Came to Me

TWO   17
To Become All Flame

THREE   27
Profound Feelings of Despair and Abandonment

FOUR   37
Drawn by the "Goddess" of Nature

FIVE   47
Traditionalists in Spite of Ourselves

SIX   55
The Stillness of the Eternal

SEVEN   65
Searching for Ourselves

EIGHT   75
Craving for Community

NINE   85
Moving for Rights to Obligations

TEN   93
Whoever Would Have Life Must Lose It

Foreword

It can't be much more than a year ago that I opened my e-mail box to find a letter from a spiritual seeker. That's not unusual; I get a couple of these most every day. But a few things about this letter made it stand out dramatically from the crowd.

In the first place, the writer was well-informed. Many who write me seem to be floundering around spiritually, reacting to ideas they've encountered in a superficial way. They have only a vague awareness of the range of alternatives that world religions present. But this correspondent had not only done an admirable amount of reading and research, she had also thought seriously about the implications and conflicting propositions of these views. She had not confined herself to familiar backyard-variety American religions, but had explored Eastern faiths as well. She'd made good progress in digesting what she'd learned, and was ready to take a new step.

In the second place, the writer was well-spoken. Often the people who write me are grappling with immense life-and-death issues, but are frustrated by a limited verbal ability that makes it hard for them to express themselves, and hard even to order their thoughts. Not so with this writer, who possessed not only clarity of thought and speech, but an engaging sense of humor. She didn't take herself too seriously, yet she was able to recognize those things that deserve serious respect. A lot of spiritual seekers have that see-saw tilted the wrong way.

But the most surprising thing about this e-mail was that the writer said she was fifteen years old. I reread the letter several times, trying to make sense of that. Could it be a typo? I forwarded the letter to some friends in the publishing field. One very knowledgeable editor wrote back to say that it was probably a scam; no one that young could write so well. But if it was true, "Sign her to a contract, quick!"

So it's with a great sense of gratification that I now page through Marjorie's work, *A Tiny Step Away from Deepest Faith*. Perhaps she was a tiny step away the day she wrote me, but at the time it seemed much farther. Marjorie was one of those seekers with a profound inner hunger for truth. In her short life she had looked for it in many forms; she had allied herself with Wicca and paganism, had for a time been an active practitioner of her family's Judaism, and now was feeling increasingly drawn to Jesus Christ. Yet she was concerned that the political views to which she was strongly committed would be incompatible with classic Christian faith. Not to mention that, of all the religious paths she might choose, becoming a Christian was the one that would make least sense to her family and peers.

Yet in *A Tiny Step* we can see that Marjorie's entry into Christianity was a natural outgrowth, rather than a rejection, of the spiritual yearnings that that had been growing in her all these years. In the process of unfolding her own journey, she opens our eyes to some of the distinctives of her generation—a generation that has so far escaped the imposition of labels, the generation that comes *after* "Generation X." Despite Baby Boomers' assumption that "young people" are all alike (that is, all like we were), we find that her generation questions and even rejects some of our treasured assumptions.

"We have ceased to believe in anything else—the utopian dreams of our parents hold no water for us, and bland ideology and trust in rationality do not keep us interested." Her generation appears, from the outside, depressed and directionless, but this is evidence of a refusal to settle for tidy, complacent satisfactions. "It's all or nothing—and if we are now stuck with nothing, it's just because we're waiting for the All."

Well, when you put it like that, it doesn't seem too unreasonable to hope that this most hip and aloof of generations could discover Jesus Christ. Marjorie stresses over and over that it's Him as a person, not an institution or a package of beliefs, that attracts her. And He's not a figure in an old story, but a living presence she can experience, whom she first encountered while gazing at His eyes in a painting, "so grave, so deep, so loving."

Becoming a Christian wasn't a matter of personal taste, as if, after sampling all the items on the menu, she decided it suited her best. She was not pulled in by the aesthetic appeal of the faith, or convinced by logical argument. As Marjorie says, "Christianity is nothing but a series of paradoxes." (I like that description; though Christian apologists are often found laboring to construct airtight logical arguments to persuade non-believers of the faith, I've always found that approach misguided.) No, Marjorie says, "I simply met Christ and I had to submit."

Though she's not yet two decades old, Marjorie is bearing testimony to the same experience Christians have tried to express for two thousand years. It's the experience of Christ as a living person—not an example, a theory, or a hero from distant history. He is a person who is eminently alive, who defines what "alive" means. The old debates about whether or not He rose from the dead suddenly seem ridiculous: of course He did, because He's here right *now*.

And this experience of the living Jesus Christ, like the experience of any person, has its own distinctive personality or flavor. In this case, it's a quality of *authority,* in the root meaning of "author," creator, the wellspring of life. I was a little older than Marjorie, and not nearly as smart or well-read, when I had a similar experience (though mine was more sudden; I could pinpoint it to a Tuesday afternoon). Like Marjorie, I would have said at the time that "if I were to choose the religion most comfortable to me, I would most likely be a Hindu, where I was gradually heading for a while before Christ found me." Like her, I was knocked sideways by the unexpected presence of a Person whom I didn't previously believe existed, but who I discovered to be the source and foundation of my life.

It's heartening to read Marjorie's story and see that God is still at work in the world in the same old way, still surprising young people with the power of His presence, still filling them with His light. Most joyous of all is realizing how this submission is the beginning of perfect freedom. At the end of all these wanderings provoked by a restless self it is possible to find a true homecoming. "Slowly, slowly, I saw everything in my being, my existence, answered by Him, everything about Him responded to who I was, what my fears were, what I hoped for, what I needed."

It takes only a tiny step to enter deepest faith, but from there on the horizon stretches to eternity.

Frederica Mathewes-Green

Introduction

"I am that star most dreaded by the wise,

for they are drawn against their will to me. . . ."

—W. H. Auden, *For the Time Being*

When I was eleven, maybe twelve, during the unhappiest period of my life, I remember being turned speechless by a painting of Christ. It's all blurry now, surreal almost, and the only thing I remember is His eyes. They were so grave, so deep, so loving; they shook me to the core. I was very hostile towards religion then, especially Christianity, but there was something about this portrait that made me ache—without realizing why, without understanding. I was sad and pathetic, and looking into those eyes, I just felt broken.

A year later I would refer to this as the time I was almost "sucked in" by the allure of Christianity, I was almost captured by the beauty of the image of Christ. "It is the stories I am drawn to—I am a writer," I would say. "It is not Christ that drew me, but the myth." From there it was a long time before I would seriously consider Christianity, before I would approach it again with that awed and longing wonder, that yearning brokenness. It would be a long time before I would give in.

After I did surrender, it became apparent how far away from my former self I was. At some point last year a girl, surprised when I said I was not religiously Jewish anymore, nor was I an atheist, asked me what my religion was. When I told her, rather sheepishly, that I was an aspiring Christian, I received a rather cryptic, comical answer: "Well, we can't help what we believe," she sighed.

There is really nothing more intellectually unfashionable than Christianity. If I could have chosen something else, I would have—God just had other plans for me. For the longest time after succumbing to what I believe is

Providence, I was embarrassed, even ashamed of what I found I believed; it was not until recently that I have been open about my faith. Even by the end of last year, when I had firmly decided to join the Orthodox Church, most people in my life assumed that I was an atheist. Maybe it was because I was an intellectual, or because I was liberal in politics—the reason does not matter.

So many people talk about my conversion as if I looked at all the religions and chose what sounded the best to me, what "fit" me the best. Far from it—if I were to choose the religion most comfortable to me, I would most likely be a Hindu, where I was gradually heading for a while before Christ found me. It wasn't a matter of finding "what worked for me"—it was an encounter with a Person. It wasn't that Christianity seemed to make the most sense out of all of them—far from it, as Christianity is nothing but a series of paradoxes—or that it was the most aesthetically pleasing. I simply met Christ and had to submit.

Four years ago God started to speak to me, and around three years ago, for the first time, I began to be struck by the Person of Christ. I who was so hostile towards anything Christian found myself devouring everything I could about this strange man and who He was—it consumed me. And slowly, slowly, I saw everything in my being, my existence, answered by Him, everything about Him responded to who I was, what my fears were, what I hoped for, what I needed.

Explaining this has always been harder, especially considering that this was a process spanning years. Over time I saw Christ becoming more and more a part of my life; I saw everything somehow relating itself to Jesus. It is so hard to communicate this worldview—to speak about my experience to those who do not have the same mindset. It is like speaking another language.

But at the heart of the matter is a universality that exists between me and my generation. I found an answer—but my questions are the same. We are an uprooted, chaotic, jaded age bracket. My favorite teacher, and probably the closest thing I have to a mentor in my life, the devoted Shakespearean Dr. Abate, said in an article in the school magazine a few years ago that when she had read the Bard in high school she did not like it—she couldn't believe that the world was as dismal as he painted it, that people could be as cruel as they are in the Shakespearean world. Students now, she went on, are less naïve—they understand Shakespeare and the world he depicts. I remember how, when I read that, it struck me—we live in a generation of rejection. It is a rebellion unlike that of our parents; we reject even their idealism. We reject everything.

This is scary, of course, for many established religious figures. Our rejection is understood as a prideful revolution against authority—including that of God. In the form that it has taken, this might well be true—but I, for one, think that it is a good sign. We flee from the lukewarm, from pat answers, from dull ideology. We've thrown out everything; we're continually emptying our hands.

It's there that God meets us, in our refusal of anything less than perfect good. God comes to us in our brokenness. Christ reached out to me in middle school when I saw Him in that portrait; I felt there a hint of grace. I was still too prejudiced then, too close-minded to let Him in. . . . I had been brainwashed to hate Him, so all I could do was stare and forget. But that lightning moment stayed in my soul—I carried it with me.

My generation is actually quite prepared for, ready for, and accepting of spirituality. We have been called godless, but this is true only in the shallowest of senses, in that most of us do not yet profess a creed, and have rejected what are viewed as traditional religious sentiments. Although our religious feelings sometimes may appear to be slipshod and badly put together, there is a sort of desperate feeling to it; there is a sense of necessity. There is a feeling that in this dark world of ours there must be hope; we reach out for it wildly. More than anything else, I think, we have ears to hear. I was open to the Truth, always searching for it, even if my prejudices tried to steer me away for a while. When I now speak to people my age and expect them to be turned off by theological questions and speculation—to be interested in passing day-to-day concerns instead of the eternal mysteries—instead, they listen, intensely, attentively. They are genuinely interested in God; they are waiting for God.

Many are even drawn to the figure of Christ. Then comes the plunge into neo-Gnosticism and other New Age strands of Christianity; many behold Christ, fall in love with Him, and simply cannot reconcile this love with what they *think* Christianity is. So many, my former self included, take Christ and what they want Him to be and create Him in their own image, attempting to take Him away from what they view as evil, hopeless, shallow. But the truth remains, and Christ, who does not see time like we do, waits patiently.

It is hard, sometimes, to remember who I am, where I came from, who I used to be. It is hard to remember how empty I was once, and what anger I had. When the burden of the responsibilities of faith seem to overwhelm me, it is hard to recall that without these duties, I was full of darkness, loneliness, and despair. I was an entirely different person two years ago: I am not who I was. This is a somber thought.

It is all very confusing and obscured, but there is no way to go back to the source of this all without again standing before the portrait of Christ, with His eyes of fire catching on to my heart. The worst is when I reduce this to ideas and theories, and forget my first love—the piercing of the heart through love of Him. I was dead, and came alive again; I was lost, and was found. This is all that is essential, both for me, and anyone my age who is empty and abandoned: this sudden contact with heavenly love that brought breath into man and gave life to my dead soul. The words may pass, but love is eternal.

The essence of all that follows in these chapters should be this, this one sense of being touched by the light of paradise. Anything that transgresses from that experience—be kind enough to ignore it, and may God forgive me my mistakes.

ONE
How God Came to Me

"It is not for man to seek, or even to believe in God.

He has only to refuse to believe in everything

that is not God. . . .

A man has only to persist in his refusal,

and one day or another God will come to him."

—Simone Weil, *On Science, Necessity, and the Love of God*

Autumn in New Jersey is mind-boggling. It's as if the golden-cherry leaves fall into the sunset and everything is haloed by silence and smoke and some distant humming. It's hard even to walk to class during the day—you don't want to go inside—and if it weren't for the biting cold I probably would just stay out. It's so beautiful it makes me ache, and that's all I can think about as my friend and I walk from the student center—beyond the grass and the trees and the rich blue sky—to go see our math grades. We are talking about faith, though the word doesn't come up.

I don't remember what sparked the conversation that day, but we were talking about our lives, about our unhappiness, about our despairs and failures. And we started talking about faith. We talked about the fact that humans are not rational creatures. We're expected to be rational, and maybe all the philosophies pushed on us indoctrinate us into thinking we are, but even as teenagers we have discovered that reason can only go so far. I talked of my paranoia that my friends didn't care for me, for example—rationally, I know that they do, but I can't apply that to my life, it is not real for me. I talked about my friends with eating disorders, who rationally know that they are not fat, that what they are doing hurts them and doesn't make their problems go away—and yet they don't know it, inside; it's not real but only dry, stale facts that exist on some other level. I started talking about my ideas on philosophy and history, and to my surprise my friend didn't look bored—she nodded vigorously—yes, yes—it's not about what we know with our reason, she agreed.

I am a person of faith, I realize, and this makes me somewhat uncomfortable, because that label has come to mean so many things. When I was younger I would have equated it with a person who was not in touch with reality, a person who relied on feelings instead of the truth. And yet for me faith is the undercurrent of everything in my life. Every breath confirms my trust—sometimes strong, sometimes wavering—in a Truth that endures, in something beyond myself. Every step I take, from the student center to the math building, is aided by the help of my belief in God. It started happening too long ago for me to really appreciate its novelty, but I find that everything I do is permeated with the words of the Nicene Creed: "I believe in one God, the Father Almighty, Maker of heaven and earth, and of all things visible and invisible; and in one Lord, Jesus Christ. . . ."

It's this sudden realization of the fullness of faith in my life that shocks me, because I remember too well the emptiness, the pointless grabbing in everyday life for something, for someone, always for some dream or person or idea that I had latched onto without knowing why. I realize that all my sadnesses now are just bittersweet, because underneath their skin is a firm conviction I never before would have considered. I talked to my friend on the phone a few days later: We, you and I, I said, are passionate creatures, we throw ourselves into things, and that comes with being lost, with emptiness, because we won't settle for anything but perfection. . . . She knows what I mean, and I wonder how many people I know would say the same thing. I expected her to not know what I was talking about—I tend to do that with people. I like to think I am unique, but when I express my feelings or beliefs I find that everyone understands what I am saying and reacts to the same things as true or meaningful. If there is any common thread, it is emptiness, it is a sense of meaninglessness, but also a deep-seated need for something more, a stretch for the beyond from millions of broken people.

To some extent I know that this is nothing new. I think of Nikolai Stavrogin in Fyodor Dostoevsky's *Demons*, and his meeting with the retired Bishop Tikhon in a chapter that never made the final cut for the book. The tortured anti-hero interrogates the old man, seeking out condemnation or solace. He asks Tikhon about Christ's words to the Laodiceans in the Revelation to John: "And to the angel of the church of the Laodiceans write, 'These things says the Amen, the Faithful and True Witness, the Beginning of the creation of God: "I know your works, that you are neither cold nor hot. I could wish you were cold or hot. So then, because you are lukewarm, and neither cold nor hot, I will vomit you out of my mouth. Because you say, 'I am rich, have become wealthy, and have need of nothing'—and do not know that you are wretched, miserable, poor, blind, and naked—"'" (Revelation

12

3:14–17) Nikolai protests; why should God favor the cold over the lukewarm? Bishop Tikhon explains—the one in the most darkness stands much closer to light than the one who doesn't care either way. . . .

The issue of faith and unbelief, of indifference and suffering and hope and despair goes back much farther than my own generation. However, I believe my generation epitomizes it. It is easy to condemn us for our lack of faith in anything, in our depression and suicide rate and self-destruction and out-of-control behavior, but it is all of this that in fact gives me the most hope for us. We have ceased to believe in anything else—the utopian dreams of our parents hold no water for us, and bland ideology and trust in rationality do not keep us interested. We are iconoclasts, throwing down everything that those before us set up to guide us.

We don't believe in simple answers. We don't believe that if we can prove a fact in a Petri dish it makes any real difference. We want something more, anything more, something that doesn't have to be anatomized, something that can be experienced. We believe in personal encounters. We believe in the human touch. We don't believe in cheap happiness, in settling for second best, in mediocre joys. It's all or nothing—and if we are now stuck with nothing, it's just because we're waiting for the All.

I don't know many lukewarm people. Most of my friends who have any religious convictions at all, like me, spent years violently searching out faith. I chased it from eighth grade to eleventh before getting hold of it, and most I know took longer than that. If we truly were a "godless" nation we wouldn't be devouring whatever we could see or read in order to find God. I cannot count the amount of times people I previously assumed to be non-religious or even anti-religious have come up and talked to me about their beliefs, or about what they wanted to believe. I never initiate the conversations, but I talk about God regularly at school, and I am taken seriously. There is a tangible thirst for faith that over a hundred years of secular humanistic bias and education have failed to erase in the hearts of youth.

I have often heard adults accuse us of being cynical, sarcastic, bitter—far too much for children, anyway. But I would be more disturbed if we weren't. It is *good* that we should reject the intellectual and cultural wasteland around us; it is *good* that we should question it and consider it unfulfilling. It is *good* that we should seek higher things, for our dwelling is in the heavens.

Nikolai Stavrogin hanged himself, though he was perfectly sane. My friend and I sit in the math building, and that memory comes into my mind without my understanding why. The more I talk to my friend, the more I realize the hypocrisy of my babbling on for ten minutes about how words and ideas and reason will never be enough to express the search for the deeper truth, which can only be expressed in love. I wish I could just go up to her and hug her—human touch is the greatest

14

thing in the world—but my social inhibitions stop me; my fears about people and friends leave me leaning against a desk, quoting my favorite philosophers.

St. Paul wrote in his letter to the Ephesian Church that faith was not something we can muster up ourselves, but the purely gracious gift of God. I feel frustrated, because I know that none can come to Christ until the Father draws him, and I can't convince anyone to be happy; I can't convince anyone "that your joy may be full" (John 15:11). I can't do anything with words or ideas, even with my beliefs. I try to remember that Jesus always spoke about love—not in its wishy-washy ideal but in its head-on, dangerous, painful, and personal reality. I try to remember that He spoke of that and not of convincing others to believe in anything.

I believe—and I now love those words—that we are ready for perfect joy. I believe that perfection exists, and Truth, in which there is no shadow of darkness, but only the blinding Light of the Transfiguration. For a long time I didn't see that, didn't experience it, but still I kept searching for it, kept reaching out for it, in so many gods and finite people. And yet I knew that they weren't enough—and that rejection brought me to God. It is only necessary to refuse to put your trust in anything but the Truth, and one day or another everything will be made perfect. I believe that, truly . . . but even as I think that I have to silence myself. It is not about ideas but about pure, unshakable faith.

15

My friend and I walk back in the autumn rosiness, looking at the sky. I believe that she, and I, and all of us, are meant for something better. And I stop talking, and simply believe.

TWO
To Become all Flame

"Lot went to Joseph and said,
'Abba, as far as I can, I keep a moderate rule, with
a little fasting, and prayer, and meditation, and
quiet: and as far as I can I try to cleanse my
heart of evil thoughts. What else should I do?'
Then the hermit stood up and spread out his hands to
heaven, and his fingers shone like ten flames of fire,
and he said, 'If you will, you can become all flame.'"
—*The Desert Fathers: Sayings of the Early Christian Monks*,
translated by Benedicta Ward

My friend Stevooo and I are both believers, but we haven't always been sure exactly what it is we believe in, and we haven't always known if that's a good or bad thing. We've both come a long way, and have traveled a lot of the same paths, entertained the same religions and ideas. We share a love for nature, a tendency to over-analyze, and a concern about the balance between ritual and spirituality. I told him once that I wish that we could have lived in Ireland fifteen hundred years ago, and he could be my *anam chara*, my soul friend, my friend to whom I'd confess my sins, my friend with whom I'd discuss my spiritual progress, the twin of my spirit. He smiles a little, but I can't see in his deep brown eyes exactly what he thinks of that—he's always looking ahead, looking for something further in, and the talk of a Christian concept, even an Irish one—he loves the Celts—always throws him off.

I believe that what Augustine wrote was true, that God has made us for Himself, and our hearts are restless until they rest in Him. I know it, and Stevooo knows it too—we're young, but we have experienced it nonethe-less—years of searching, meditating, hoping, trying to find anything that would fill the void that we have tried to grown accustomed to for far too long.

Stevooo and I do come from the same general path. By the end of ninth grade, I had just barely accepted the idea of a Creator God (gender-neutral of course), and I was still a long way from anything that could resemble peace of soul. My ideas of God were vague, contradictory, and hybridized. I suppose they were a cross between Deism and pantheism—on one hand I maintained that God was impersonal, that the Supreme Being did not think, was not a Being, could not possibly care about the lives of human beings, and on the other hand I insisted that matter was somehow an emanation of God. And then I turned around again and asserted that material existence needed to be destroyed through inner knowledge of the God within. Why I needed to find the God within in order to reach a state of perfection when God was clearly also *without*, being all things, was something I never addressed. God could not be a personal God, of course, as I assumed personal meant somehow comprehensible. Christians worshiped a cardboard God, an external God, a distant, transcendent Father figure who either hated the earth or ignored it. Of course, I myself was creating a god who simultaneously hated matter and ignored it, but the irony didn't hit me at the time.

I thought I was being original. I wasn't. Daily I meet people with the same new and creative beliefs, the same delusions and contradictions I put to rest not so long ago. Stevooo doesn't know exactly what he believes yet, and his beliefs, too, flounder, change quickly, and just seem to miss something that could give him peace. The surprising thing about the beliefs of my generation is that we are *not* stupid, that it makes no sense for us to believe in such internally inconsistent philosophies, our beliefs mysterious but contradicting. We reach out at the flotsam and jetsam of spiritual speculations and grab whatever we can, holding on tightly as if attempting to catch onto a rope in the midst of hostile waters. Our spirituality isn't that of rational beings, but of drowning souls.

So we all aspire to be mystics. Our faith isn't rational; we want something that transcends reason. Because we are in a crisis, theological abstractions and scholastic reasoning seem irrelevant and distant to us; stale, bland, and useless. We are convinced that there is a great deal at stake. We are convinced that there must be a greater being than any of us can imagine—either inside us or part of us in the deepest, most unfamiliar parts of our souls.

In eighth grade I learned to believe in love, and in ninth I learned to believe that love needs guidance. My love for God was wild and frenzied, raw and confused, when I wasn't even sure what I thought of Him. I certainly wasn't thinking of Christianity yet; I wasn't even considering the Judaism of my childhood. Neo-Wicca hadn't supplied me with what I needed, and by the end of ninth grade that was as distant to me as my atheistic tendencies of the year before. I simply prayed for whatever was out there, whatever pantheon, spirit, or Ultimate Reality, to reveal itself to me. Within time, the only religion I had never considered—had always been repelled from— would become home to me.

It started gradually, using stepping stones of Christian mysticism. Neo-Gnosticism was the first, but a study of history soon left me estranged from that. Thomas Merton, and then St. Teresa of Avila, St. John of the Cross, St. Thérèse of Lisieux, St. Augustine . . . for me, the path to orthodoxy is helplessly intertwined with the authors I approached. I cannot separate Merton in my mind from my skeptical appreciation of Catholic mysticism, and Augustine is locked in with my final acceptance of Scripture as an always true, if not literal, source. After Augustine, I tend to be able to think of the authors without these connotations—by then my faith was sealed, immovable, and quite a betrayal of my earlier beliefs. I can't help realizing that if I had looked two years into the future in ninth grade, I would be shocked and appalled. But the process was completely natural. No one tried to convert me, and if they had I would not have listened. No one gave me a pamphlet or even suggested that I read about the religion. I came to it on my own terms, very stubbornly and slowly.

And the distinct feature of my beliefs has always been a mystic leaning, the concept of direct communion with a transcendent and yet omnipresent Reality, whether through meditation or ritual. In fact, this is the distinct feature of the beliefs of most spiritually oriented people of my age. This is not, in essence, something new—since the Sixties the youth culture has gone toward the Eastern religions, toward meditation, toward the Ultimate Reality, toward incense and chanting and some sort of deep communion. But there's something different about it now.

21

My parents are both loyal children of the Sixties. They never shed their activist liberalism, especially my mother, and my sisters and I grew up environmentally and socially aware, and even more than that, convinced that there could be no greater evil on this earth than government in the pocket of big business. Nixon, Reagan, and Bush were names one did not dare to speak during my childhood, and my sisters and I called each other Republicans if we were really mad.

When I ask my parents about growing up, about youth culture and youth rebellion of their era, I get a picture of something very different from that of today. I get a picture of young people who felt betrayed and cynical about the establishment—that much is the same—but I also get a picture of idealists, of people who really believed there was going to be a peaceful revolution that would radically change the nation, people who believed that love, justice, and peace would win out in the long run. I can't think of more than a handful of people who feel that way now. Cynicism does not fuel agitation for change, as it did then, but instead brings a state of apathy. We've seen people try to change things, and it's never worked, so we don't see why we should bother. My generation doesn't vote, and doesn't care. This does not just extend to politics— the world itself is seen as a fundamentally evil place, even hopeless. And yet we hope.

I believe that Christian mysticism is perhaps the only tradition suitable to our condition. Without it, we risk

22

becoming either too dependent on the world, or too adverse to it, declaring all existence as wrong and evil. Sometimes we run the risk of being both things simultaneously. Only Christianity's historical spirituality allows for the essential goodness of the world with the right balance of rejection of it as it is. "Everything God created is good"—but everything, also, is fallen. I struggled for so long—as many of my friends do now—between love of the world around us and rejection of it. My most profound moments are spent completely inactive, staring at the sky, the sea, or in my backyard doting on the spring-born peonies. . . . It is all so very beautiful and good, and it seems such a contradiction that the world of such great and inconceivable beauty is the same world of such seemingly insurmountable evil. As a believer in Christ, however, I know this is only to be expected—we live in the aftermath of a cosmic explosion of death and sin, in a world that was created not for darkness but for shining like the sun. And yet God—ineffable, inconceivable, mysterious, and always moving, acting, touching us in ways we cannot understand—has taken on this material existence for Himself, joining the divine and human natures inseparably in the Incarnation. It took me a long time to find the beauty of that paradox, and to exclaim with absurd joy to the risen God-man: "Glory to You!"

I sit on the couch with my head resting on Stevooo's chest, and I think of the Beloved Disciple doing the same to Christ the night He was betrayed. I know that Stevooo would love the Gospel of John, the spiritual Gospel, but there's no way I can think to recommend it to him without offending him. I hear his rejections of Christianity, and that of all my other non-Christian friends. One is that it seems too external, too focused on God as "other." Neo-Gnostic writers epitomize this feeling—their ancient heroes seem to be set in opposition not to the Christians of that time period, but to the Christians of today, especially some American Protestants, with a general lack of spirituality and a rationalist interpretation of faith.

I understand his objections and held them once as well, and I know that, for me, it wasn't convincing arguments that swayed me, but direct experience with what I feel is the Truth. So I defend myself, but I don't try to proselytize. I know in my heart that God is not altogether external but completely immanent in Creation, always and continually transfiguring it into the life of the world to come. But these are just words, and it frustrates me that I cannot communicate my spirituality better to others.

"I can't believe in heaven," my friend says, as our eyes fall on the beginning of a sunset. I feel calm and warm, and the red-yellow light of the sky comforts me even at the hurt I feel because of this statement.

"Most people don't know what heaven is, only some simplified version of it that they've been taught," I reply, a little too sensitively, and take his hand in mine to show that I am not offended by anything he is saying.

He nods. It all just seems too small to him, though, and I understand that. The God he has been brought up to accept as the Christian God is too small, too vengeful, too human, and too far away. He sees God here—he only can believe in a God who is closer to us than our very selves. He can only believe in a God who wishes for us to become divine, to become deified. I want to explain to him that I agree, and I want to give him every book on contemplation and hesychasm (the practice of inner silence) and meditation and deification that I own. I want to show him how I view God, and I try to show him as much as I can by just sharing my opinions when we talk. And still, he can't hear it from me, and he will hear it in his own way, not through my ideas, but through his own direct, mystical experience. I know that I can't rush the Spirit, and so I just touch him, I hug him, kiss his forehead, and hope that some of the rest I have found in Him can be given to Him even just by this.

His dark brown eyes close to the sunset, and he thinks about a God like a lightning bolt, pouring down on the earth through rain and sky and fire, moving him into a profound union, to be transformed into something that can understand Him. I lay my head back down on his chest, listen to the reassuring heartbeat, and hope he knows this means that I agree.

THREE
Profound Feelings of Despair and Abandonment

"By this attitude of complete renunciation you
shall be freed from the bondage. . . .
You shall be liberated, and come to Me."

—*The Bhagavad-Gita* 9:28

I was trying to pull the English
muffins out of the toaster when my
mom abruptly changed the topic:

"By the way, just so you don't say we never tell you any-thing"—they never tell me anything—"Jessie's starting therapy."

I turn around.

"What?"

I had no doubt that my little sister, Jessica, was unhappy, but it had been so long since my older sister, Rachel, and I had left therapy that it seemed odd to me that this should start up again. Rachel and I dealt with our depression in our own ways, and have since matured, but Jessie's was quieter, less explicit.

"She went to the guidance counselor and said she was suicidal and was cutting herself."

"She's not cutting herself. She wears short sleeves and I've seen her legs."

"I know," Mom replied as she sat down at the table.

I turned back for the English muffins, and reached for a knife to spread the peanut butter.

"I think she's just unhappy," I decided, my finger touching the blunt edge of the metal in my hand, "just like everyone else."

My mom nods because it's true, and the conversation trails off.

Later that night, I go over a mental list of all the happy people that I know. I try to think of someone my age not tainted by a sort of existential angst, not attempting to cope with profound feelings of despair and abandonment. The few I can think of I don't know well enough to be sure of. It suddenly hits me that I don't know happy people, that many of my friendships are based entirely on solidarity in a bizarre epidemic of misery. I realize that I have become happier lately—or rather, at peace—and yet this has only led to listening to my friends vent more. My newfound stability has only served to show me how lost everyone is, and how unstable all the people who are close to me are.

We aren't happy. We take Zoloft and cut open our flesh and do anything to assure us that we're here, that we feel, that our experience is valid and tangible. There's something sick in a culture where prosperity is chased by suicide. We're bored and lonely and we don't care about anything anymore, while we still worship everything. Our emotions are not silly and they are not immature. On the contrary, they are surprisingly mature, and though not all of us have the eloquence to describe the depth of our feelings, nevertheless we feel strongly and in pure concentrations. The problem is not, as has been posited, that we are shallow, but that we cannot be shallow, that our inner experience is too strong to deny; too loud and too demanding.

The teenage years are always years of turmoil. Adolescence has always been a hard time to deal with, so nothing I'm saying is original. But teens today have what other generations had, only we have it in excess, with some of the exceptional even becoming the norm. We kill ourselves more, we take more drugs and more potent drugs than our parents did. Drugs, suicide attempts, promiscuous sex—it is all an attempt to escape the world around us. Self-mutilation is rampant. In my most despairing days I took the kitchen knife and applied it on myself—never as seriously as with others I know, but because I was empty, unhappy, always wanting to go for the extremes in order to escape the hell I was in. And that's how our generation is—obsession with self-esteem and body image just serves to mirror the fact that, as my friend Lauren once told me, "We all hate ourselves and think we're fat and ugly."

Christians of all time periods have experienced this sorrow of the world, the shadow of the evil one—the hardest foe to overcome, as it has to do with the self. "There is a useful sorrow," reflected Amma Syncletica of the Desert Fathers, "and a destructive sorrow. Sorrow is useful when we weep for our sins, and for our neighbor's ignorance, and so that we may not relax our purpose to attain to true goodness, these are the real kinds of sorrow. Our enemy adds something to this. For he sends sorrow without reason, which is something called lethargy. We ought always to drive out a sadness like that with prayers and psalms."

Amma Syncletica went out into the desert to meet God. John the Baptist grew up there, and Jesus overcame Satan in its midst. Yet mindless wandering and golden calves are found there too, in an environment of true aridity. God lives there, and so does the devil. The desert is the holy land because there is nothing. Nothing but you,

30

your cross, and Christ. Evil is there too, and temptation. But we all come out into the desert to be saved.

Being a teenager is, in a sense, to be deserted—the world of childhood no longer applies and yet it is impossible to face reality yet. It is a time when despair, confusion, and loneliness are intensified—it is a great spiritual drought, and it is in the greatest spiritual drought that we find God. He comes to us in the most profound sadness, in the most unspeakable grief. He wipes away every tear from our eyes and gives us hope, and we know Him because we have been brought into the depths.

My generation is ready for Him.

My friends tell me they're empty, and I don't know what to say. I know what it's like to be empty. Our god is the person or thing we think the most about—whether it be God Himself or a crush or a celebrity or a cause or a book or an object or an ideology. My friends and I chose to worship anything—everything—in order to fill the gap that leaves us empty and unfulfilled. We are made to have every desire satisfied, and it is for this purpose that we have been born. But in a world without direction, worldly sorrow devours us who are slaves to those who by nature are not gods.

I've come out into the desert to meet God. To some, this looks like escape from the world—my beliefs, a break from reality; my aspirations, unrealistic and avoidant. But this is an escape from hell to real life, and life in abundance. I've come alone; I've left everything behind, everyone whom I previously worshiped, everything that I have been attached to. Silently and cautiously I have fallen before His cross, the sky bruised with a sunset and the ground harsh and uninviting. I have fled from the crowd to venerate an instrument of a painful and terrible death, and to find peace in the injustice of the death of my God. I have come here not to greet favors, security, or consolations. I have come here to share in this death, not because I want anything but because I love Him, and because He loves me.

When I cry, my grief is deeper than it has ever been, and yet I am not depressed. Though I am constantly at war, I am not afraid. I am not always happy, but I am drenched in wisdom and truth.

So I explain this to my friends. I tell them that I'm not unhappy anymore—sometimes I'm stressed, but I have a constant presence with me, a constant escape that isn't desperate, isn't chaotic, but is the only thing that is real. Now that I have found it it, I realize that everything *else* seems like an escape to me; everything else seems like shadows and illusions compared to the very real experience of encountering God. It's very real, and very personal, close to me and, more than that, inside me. After her conversion, the writer Anne Lamott wrote: "I had no big theological thoughts but had discovered that if I said, Hello?, to God, I could *feel* God say, Hello, back. It was like being in a relationship with Casper.

Sometimes I wadded up a Kleenex and held it tightly in one fist so that it felt like I was walking hand in hand with him."

I want other people to be happy. I tell my friends who are religious or spiritual but haven't yet found anything like this to wait, to pray, to meditate, to try to clear their minds of whatever is blocking them from their own happiness. Often, it's stress—school, with its homework keeping us up till 3 AM, or people, relationships, parents. And to older people, it all sounds so trivial! Here we are, comfortable, affluent, well-fed, even bored, and we couldn't be more miserable. Do adults understand this? I like to think that they at least wonder about it, whatever answers they come up with. Most adults seem surprised, even shocked by the depth of emotion that people my age experience. We're not always eloquent, but we get across the message in scars and suicide attempts and overdoses.

When my older sister was depressed, she swallowed a bottle of antidepressants. She didn't get her stomach pumped, but she did have to drink charcoal. She then spent another week in Charter, the mental hospital. I had already been there once. I asked her, later on, after this all was past, if she really wanted to commit suicide. "No," she shrugged.

That's the society we live in.

I watch my younger sister carefully. I've been cruel to her at times, like all sisters, and I feel bad about it. I don't

33

want her to be depressed—and not for the right reasons. Not because I love her—though I do—but because she's taking my identity away, *my* depression, *my* suicidal thoughts, *my* cutting. They're not mine for the keeping anymore, but they're still part of me, in my mental junkyard, somewhere in front of what little childhood memories I have and behind all the mindless stress of high school.

I sit with her and watch our mutual favorite show, *Degrassi: The Next Generation*. You can't do much better than a Canadian teenage soap opera. It's an episode about cutting, overdramatic and simplified as always. Ellie sobs as she thrusts the sharp point of a compass into her skin.

"You *have* to talk to someone aboot this," Paige, who has witnessed Ellie cutting, insists, with her characteristic Canadian accent.

I look at Jessie, who seems to be intensely following the plotline.

The problem is that our lives aren't like this; they aren't solved in thirty minutes. We don't talk to Paige who sends us to the counselor's office where everything becomes okay. It's not superficial; it's something ingrained in us. If the adults who write the show think that Ellie is cutting because her dad is in the army, or because her mom is an alcoholic, or because she's failing math (yes, it really is a soap opera), they're sorely mistaken. It's not the external things that bother us. If it were, there would be no reason to be unhappy. Maybe a little stressed, a little irritated sometimes—but that's not the problem at all. The problem is an intense hunger inside us for something we haven't learned to understand yet, haven't encountered.

I want to tell Jessie that things aren't as bad as they seem. Things will get easier. I want to show her the sunset outside, and how the rose tint fades into indigo, and how the stars in winter shine like tiny, icy flames. I want to tell her that I'm sorry, and I wish I could lend her some of my own peace, just a taste to know that it's real. I wish I could take some of her sadness and give it to my parents, give it to my teachers, just a taste so they can know that it, too, is completely real. And I want to go outside and look at the stars and forget about the cold, and just pray.

It's cold, and I remember something that happened at the end of sophomore year, towards summer. I'm at a friend's Sweet Sixteen party. I'm not a party person, really; I don't work well with crowds. I wouldn't be here except that I care about this friend a lot, but I'm starting to regret coming after a half hour or so. I talk a little with some people, but feel kind of out of it. I don't like dancing, and I don't like drinking, which is all that my friend Brian is doing. The party is outdoors, in a tent set up outside a country club. I wander outside for a bit, and walk into the parking lot, alone, thinking.

It has been a hard year for me emotionally. It is getting better, and I am just beginning to realize that I am indeed a happy person compared to most people I knew. At school I'm not, because of stress. Outside of school, a certain peace fills me with an inexplicable feeling of joy.

I look heavenward, and I'm knocked out by the color of the sky towards the end of the sunset, dark pink and purple falling into black. I see how beautiful the full moon can be, and I fall to my knees. Next to me is a telephone pole, and I'm suddenly stricken by how similar telephone poles look to crosses. I can still hear the music from the tent, soft and rhythmic, drawing the whole landscape into an undeniable pulse.

Inside, they dance, and some of them sit, bored, unhappy. I am on the ground by a telephone pole, on my knees, crying a little, softly. My eyes turn upward, and I remember every unhappiness I've felt since sixth grade, and before that, even. I feel a little anxious, but I know everything will be all right. I am a different creature than I was before, and this is a scary thought, but a pretty one.

So I pray at the foot of a cross. And the sunset fades into darkness, and my classmates inside the tent keep dancing as the music keeps pulsing. Do they wonder where I am? I ask myself, but I know they've already forgotten about me. They will come out eventually. I cross myself, and wait for my mother to pick me up.

FOUR

Drawn by the "Goddess" of Nature

"The heavens praise Thee, and their whole might,

the sun, the moon, and all the choir of stars,

the earth, the sea and all that therein is,

the heavenly Jerusalem, the Church of the firstborn

that stands written upon the heavens. . . ."

—from the *Divine Liturgy of St. James*

In the spring of eighth grade I started to believe in love. It wasn't that I fell in love with someone; it wasn't that I realized how much I loved others in my life. I started to believe in a Higher Power first, and it softened my heart like wax—and suddenly I realized I couldn't help believing in love.

It was in spring that I fell in love with peonies. We have a few garden plots in our backyard, and when April comes around it's really beautiful—but nothing in the plots compares to the peonies. The white ones bloom first, then the pink—huge, ornate, fragrant, flowing, pure like water, soft like silk, dazzling like light.

I can't remember exactly what opened my eyes. But a few things spark in my memory: It was halfway through eighth grade when my beloved English teacher, Mrs. Hannon, recommended a book to me—*The Mists of Avalon*. I bought it, and it changed my life, just as it has changed the life of many people my age.

The book opened my soul to a hunger for beauty. It's obvious why the book itself is so popular—the characters are vividly described and the plot is enchanting. I love what Marion Zimmer Bradley, a woman who was buried a Christian, did with the Arthurian myths. It is not, however, historically accurate—the Celts did not worship the gods as Bradley portrays them, nor did the Christians of the time worship Christ as Bradley portrays Him. But this does not really matter, and it most certainly did not matter for me that spring—all I knew is that my atheism crumbled away as soon as I realized how beautiful Creation is, how good life can be when everything you see is touched by an otherworldly light.

The book is especially popular among teen neo-Wiccans, and I quickly became one of the fold. The book opened my eyes to Divine Mystery, to an Unknown Force showering love over a Creation that spilled to the brim with blessings and adoration. The book helped me fall in love with nature, with harmony, with love, joy, peace, patience, kindness, goodness, faithfulness, gentleness, and self-control—everything Paul praised in Galatians 5. I had a name for all of this: *Goddess*.

I was galvanized. This is what I had been looking for, this is what I had been searching for in friends and idealism and my dreams. Here it was: a living faith, a mystical faith, a celebration of life and humanity and sacred love so precious and so pure, passed down in secret and in patience for thousands of years. I had found a path of transformation and of joy, a faith where the entire self was permeated with a stillness beyond all action, the Source of All Being. I felt loved; I felt illumined. I could not remember how I ever thought that love was just an illusion for books and fantasies—here was love, for me, in this Power, in this indescribable force.

There is a lot of confusion on all sides as to what my then-adopted creed really was; Wicca is neither Satan worship nor the oldest religion in the world. Wicca is fifty years old, a reconstructionist religion pieced together from modern sentiments and attitudes and memories of ancient religions. It is a desperate celebration of beauty in a sterile world; that is why so many are drawn to it. I know why I was—I badly needed faith in beauty and goodness and mystical light; it was a sickness.

How can I fault my peers for turning to paganism? The earth is our mother. I still feel closest to God outside, and no poem or song has moved me more than the sky, than the stars, than the clouds, the trees, or the little violets blossoming over the moss of my backyard. Many of my friends are pagans, some are even Wiccans. A great many of them express an intense concern to be closer to the earth, and profess that the "Judeo-Christian attitude of domination over the earth" has led to the environmental problems in our world today.

Why this emphasis on nature? Why does every spiritual person I know care deeply about the earth, about animals, about Creation? Speaking from experience, I can only say that its attraction lies in its purity, in its perfect reality in the light of so much artificiality. Maybe it is a subconscious reaction to hundreds of years of enlightenment, science and rationalism. Maybe it's just that the world is dying, and the Spirit can't bear it. Maybe it's just that we know that we're sick, and we want something clear, pure, true.

I never really saw any Christians defend the earth with love, so everything I thought about the destructive Judeo-Christian tradition seemed plausible. Christian

40

leaders have not responded to Apollo with St. Francis's "Brother Sun"; they have not responded to an intense love of animals with St. Seraphim's bear; they have not responded to pantheism with a healthy view of God's love for Creation. Most older Christians have failed to see the obvious: that love for nature means that we are searching for something more. Frantic earth worship is better than lukewarm belief; it means that we want something, need something—teenagers know that they need *something*. The fact that this "something" is identified with the earth, something more than humanity, something mysterious and beautiful, is a good thing.

I began to believe in God because I felt that I needed to. Not a Creator God, and definitely not one that could be called "Father." Back in eighth grade, my beliefs weren't completely formed—I didn't study my beliefs extensively, and I couldn't even finish a non-fiction book on the topic. But I knew that when I went outside something spoke to me. For the first time I felt a little happiness that I'd been searching for, a little joy outside the love of friends and family that I needed so much. It wasn't so much what I believed in but that I believed, dangerously and explicitly, in something beyond myself. The liberating experience of faith haunted me for the next two years as I searched for something more substantial to put my trust in.

At the time, I just let my faith be in peonies. I'd spend hours outside, thinking, in front of them, loving, smiling— the beautiful white peonies with the soft, soft petals, like angel's wings. I kissed them with the reverence I now give to icons, and it felt just as real. I knew that inside, I would go online for hours, and watch some TV, debate some politics. And I knew that I would never feel real except outside, in the light or in the stars.

Was that wrong? There was definitely some idolatry involved, but I don't believe that I was led there by mistake. Without that spring in eighth grade I never would have turned inward, I never would have found the only One who matters to me. I wouldn't believe in love, and I wouldn't believe in God. Maybe I called it "Goddess" back then, but all I meant was that the light on the peonies was beautiful, and I wanted to love whatever created it passionately and exclusively. I knew even then that nothing else would make me happy.

I did not care about beliefs, really, when I was Wiccan; that wasn't what was important. The spirituality and its power was what drove me—not the revelation of Truth. I welcomed the fact that so much of neo-Wicca was choosing aspects from all the world's spiritual traditions, and just holding on to it all, trying always to feel, to reach, to touch beyond. The Celtic gods were obvious for me, but I also valued and viewed other pantheons as other "aspects" of the Divine. I accepted karma, of course not from the Celtic tradition or even what one would generally view as the "pagan" tradition. The yin and the yang, the ankh, runes—I took them all as part of a pan-pagan heritage, and the diversity of it all was necessary for me at the time. Nothing had grabbed me yet, so I was grabbing.

I tried to live for years on the precept that I could live on bread alone, and it failed. And that's when paganism came into the picture for me; it is our generation's admission that life outside of the Spirit is an absurdity, that we are primarily supplicants—that is our function. My generation knows that we need something beyond ourselves; we know that they need something. Where better to start than Creation? The first religions were nature-based, and that prepared them for Christ, who is the Source of all Life.

When I was Wiccan I had many gods, but they didn't really matter to me except that they were gods. Any gods would have done; I just needed something to explain the passionate love I felt for the earth, the sea, the sky. The summer after eighth grade my family went to England, and Tintagel was the most beautiful place I had ever visited. Afterwards, in ninth grade—still pagan, no longer Wiccan—I wrote about the experience: "Yes, I suppose, looking back, I was one of those dime-a-dozen teen pagans. . . . Then again, I never gave a name to my gods, I never worshiped anything besides for the power which I recognized in the unresponsive slate gray sky, or the flowing of blue-green waters uncovering a seashell, or how light lingers around the maples and pines of my backyard in the fog of the morning. . . . That was all I knew and all I claimed to know. I never claimed to be a worker of 'magick.' The closest I ever came to that was whispering a prayer of healing every now and then outside to the distant moon, haloed in the dark blue of the fading twilight." I went on, "I was not completely sure about the religion I had chosen. One thing I *was* sure of, though, was how deeply I was moved by the picture of this land, the rock and the water, the land and the sea . . . all blue and green and mountains of gray. . . ."

My friend Stevooo, about whom I've written before, says that his main barrier to Christianity is the fact that it cannot accept the earth as divine. Like me, his major religious experiences were outdoors, in nature, and I try to explain to him the distinction between the Christian and the pagan view of Creation and why I accept the former. I explain how Creation, while beautiful, needs God, needs One who is beyond Creation, and on some level he understands what I'm saying, accepts what I'm saying, but he can't get beyond that fine line, where God is in the world but is not the world.

Even so, nature led me to God. Looking out to the endless waters of Tintagel, I knew that there had to be something more. I knew that it wasn't enough, and I felt my soaring heart lower itself into emptiness. I knew that the earth wasn't eternal, and that hurt me, it pierced me where I had just been filled with love. "That couldn't be ephemeral," I wrote, trying to recapture the moment, "it couldn't! It all had to be deep, forever, enormous, unending. . . ."

I found what I needed in the earth—something to believe in, something to love. And it led me away from worship of it. One of the truest things I ever read was the oft-quoted passage in Augustine's *Confessions*: "When I asked the earth, it responded: 'I am not God.' When I asked the heavens, the sun, the moon, the stars, they said: 'Nor are we the God you seek.' I said: 'Speak to me of my God.' Loudly, they exclaimed: 'It is He Who made us.' The heavens, the earth, and everything that is in them, all these things tell me to love you." When I read this, I stared at the words with a simple joy, knowing that this was exactly what had happened to me. Nature had been my answer—and my generation's answer—to the stifling reality of human evil, of artificiality, of the modern age. And nature's answer to me had been God.

It occurs to me as I'm writing this that the peonies haven't bloomed yet. I'm praying they bloom by Monday so that I can give one to my friend Christine for her birthday. I want to give her something that I love more than myself—something that taught me how to love. I believe in miracles now, and I believe that if I walk outside the peonies could bloom in the twinkling of an eye, burst open in pure, colorless light. It's not God, but it was my first step to Him. And I believe in less obvious miracles; I believe that peonies are enough to bring any lifeless heart to the Creator of creation.

FIVE

Traditionalists in Spite of Ourselves

"Every care should be taken to hold fast
to what has been believed everywhere,
always, and by all."

—St. Vincent of Lerins

There was a rather brief period of my life when I was actually a religious Jew—when I was little I was very proud of my Jewish heritage and even vaguely believed in the Jewish G-d my Hebrew teachers taught and about whom my parents never talked. We went to our Reform synagogue the first Friday of every month at the least, and my parents found it very important to bring us up as Jews, keeping generally kosher (I've never had lobster or pork) and having a Shabbat dinner almost every week. There were lots of rituals, and lots of holidays, but we were not really believing Jews, so to speak. It wasn't until fourth grade that I really started to believe, although faith was by no means the center of my life. I remember taking my mother's Orthodox prayer book—she had converted in a Conservative synagogue—from our Jewish bookshelf to the right of the TV in the family room, and reading the prayers with interest, sounding them out in Hebrew first, the harsh tone of the Semitic language full of strength and faith and brute force: "*Modeh ani lifanecha, melech chai nikayam*, I render thanks unto thee, everlasting King. . . ." I kept the book by my bed so that I could do the morning prayers when I woke up—they had prayers for everything, even washing hands! To me this seemed amazing, that prayer would grace all things—looking back I would say that I had a sacramental mindset. Of course, I didn't know that washing hands was actually an important ceremony historically in Judaism. When it came to traditional rituals in Judaism I had a sort of diluted version; we replaced *tefillin* with process theology. Although I do remember

48

belief in God, I never believed in a God who spoke through prophets, or a God who had a people and ancient scrolls. Only the Orthodox Jews believed in that, those oddly dressed men and women who still believed in a messiah and who started fights with Reform Jews at the Western Wall.

And yet, at ten years old, I'd wake up and face east, and pray, "*Shema yisra'el adonai elohaynu adonai echad*," and the pattern would flow through me, knowing that others were praying with me, had prayed like this for thousands of years. I didn't put things like this into words, then, and now I can, but I'd rather not. It wouldn't be honest. I had no intellectual pretensions about the matter, no philosophical or theological justification. I had not read Maimonides, and I did not know who Abraham Joshua Heschel was. And yet I prayed because I needed that connection. It was ancient, but not ossified; it was old, but it was alive to me. I didn't know what I was saying; I didn't know who God was. I didn't know the prayers I was praying were Orthodox Jewish prayers. All I knew was that I wanted to pray, not just my own words but the words of thousands of years speaking through me.

I couldn't just live by this feeling anymore as I got older—I needed to create reasons for myself. When I first looked into Wicca in eighth grade one of the main things that drew me to it was its assurance of being ancient. Teen pagans—my former self included—will usually confront you with a charge about Wicca being the oldest religion in the world—older than Christianity, of course, but even older than the other major world religions too. Of course, a casual observer might note that Wicca as such did not exist until the mid-twentieth century, and has undergone a great deal of change even since then. This is not, however, necessarily a bad thing. Why does it matter if Wicca is old or not? If it is right, isn't that good enough? Wouldn't it be better to be new and fresh in the first place?

The fact is that new and fresh is not what we are looking for. We are traditionalists despite ourselves. The New Age would have no followers if it were not able to convince its majority that it is, in fact, a revival of the Exceedingly Old Age. We *like* rituals; we just are sick of the formulas we're accustomed to. We *like* traditions; we just don't believe in the traditions we were brought up with. The question isn't a matter of whether we are looking for something new or old; the question is a matter of life. The example used before, that of Wicca, exemplifies this. Wicca, a follower of Silver Ravenwolf would assure you, is thousands of years old. Wicca, he—or, most likely, she—would go on, was often persecuted, and often misunderstood. Wicca, our teacher would say, was a carrier of wisdom and grace in times of foolishness and darkness. In short, teen pagans' history of their faith is the same as that of most any other religion. Despite the fears and anxieties of many parents over such witchcraft and evil, almost every Wiccan is simply doing what every generation has done, what every spiritually hungry person has done, what every heart and mind has done in the history of humanity. Their adversary—though as I am assured daily without actually asking, *Wiccans do not believe in the devil!*—reasonably enough, is the same enemy that every great religion has always faced—staleness, blandness, boredom, a lack of wonder in the face of an infinitely awesome universe. The question is a matter of whether or not one can look out and see the golden light of the summer sunset as it falls on the trees and ivy. The question is not about structure and traditions but the presence or absence of life.

Rituals are often thought of as hindering spirituality, but that has never been true for me. When I was searching for spirituality I searched for more ritual and more tradition, more "spiritual" practices: more spells, prayers, incantations, Gnostic rosaries, prostrations, recipes, amulets, and accessories. The private longing of the heart needs to be supplemented by something tangible, something tested, tried, and true, something lost to us: Everyone instinctually knows that we have lost our way somehow. As a ten–year-old in my bedroom, feeling something but not knowing what, my own words and thoughts seemed irrelevant. All I could do was hold onto the prayers written in large black letters of a strange language of a timeworn people.

My parents came from a generation when it made sense to be a Reform Jew, when protesting was always a good thing, when everything was changing and people believed in youth. After all the destruction passed it seems that all anyone wanted was to meekly crawl back to what we thought was archaic and turned out to be essential. In the confusion, it seems, we've given it all another name, hidden it under different forms, called it ancient mysticism, ancient paganism, ancient Gnosticism, ancient mystery religions, ancient divination, ancient prayers, ancient practices. The practices usually aren't ancient, but the point is that we are searching for an ancient faith.

My morning prayers have changed a bit since childhood—still Orthodox, but Christian this time, strangely familiar, with the same archaic English translation from an ancient tongue: "*Doxa si, Kyrie, doxa si,* glory to Thee, O Lord, glory to Thee. . . ." I gush about the liturgy, over a thousand years old, to whoever will listen—the young Catholics disillusioned with the modernization of Vatican II, the pagans who have by some stroke of fate become interested in the chants of Hildegard von Bingen, Christians of various denominations sick of contemporary Christian music that can sound more like love ballads than hymns of worship. It's not essential—of course: What is essential is that I believe in "the humanity of God," the historical Incarnation of God the Word. Yet in doing this Christ has sanctified Creation and human history along with it. Those who have experienced Him have been transformed, and so has human history. I call this Tradition. Not traditions, rituals, routine, and simply going through the motions—these exist in every religion—but the ancient "faith which was once for all delivered to the saints" (Jude 1:3). I am so small, and the thoughts and beliefs and practices of human history are so much larger than I can approach or understand. The only thing that matters to me is Christ, and there are two thousand years of failures and triumphs when it comes to knowing Him. I approach such history with fear and trembling.

Yet all in all I have to remember that whatever philosophizing I do, ultimately it is meaningless. What matters is that feeling I felt when I prayed the morning hymns, wanting to be part of something beyond myself, not knowing how to express myself adequately. That's what my peers are feeling.

I stopped being a Wiccan when I looked into the history of the religion. I stopped being a pagan because I was simply believing in my own personal fancies, my own ideas, and my God was as small as I was. I wanted something larger. I waited for a pantheon—any pantheon—to take hold of me. Any religion of old, any forgotten wisdom, any god or goddess willing to grab me. To my utter dismay, I began to feel the Christian "pantheon" drawing me in—Jesus, Mary, the Magdalene . . . I stuck with Gnosticism until I looked into the history of *that* as well. In time I realized what ancient faith I was looking for, what religion, what Tradition, what Person. It—He—was not what I wanted. But I was looking for Truth.

My Jewish childhood prepared me for a lot of things. Of course it prepared me for traditional Christianity when I finally came to Him, as traditional Christianity comes directly out of Judaism. But above all Judaism gave me a sense of tradition—of history understood as a process of following the One True God. Ancient prayers, written for me, soaked in thousand-year-old wisdom—my childhood is full of rituals and prayers, Shabbat candles and Torah scrolls, Kiddush cups and braided bread, although none of this was explained to me very well—and this sensibility carried me through to the rest of my life until now. When I cross myself, bow, kiss my icons in the morning, and pray—*O Heavenly King, O Comforter, the Spirit of Truth who art in all places and fillest all things, the treasury of good things and the Giver of Life*—I sometimes remember this, where I came from. Everything I had then is not gone, but has been fulfilled—abundantly.

SIX

The Stillness of the Eternal

"Truly, if such are the good things of this
time, what will be those of eternity?
If such is the beauty of visible things,
what shall we think of invisible things?
—St. Basil the Great, *The Hexaemeron*

I want to talk about *forever*, and I
keep getting the picture in my

mind of the summer before eleventh grade, at Block Island, when I started thinking about eternity. It wasn't more than a year ago, but something about the image in my mind is timeless—the light on the water, sitting on the rocks, trying to grasp something, somewhere just beyond what I could see, the sky endless and my feet bare on the sharp curves of the wet ground.

I was reading St. Teresa of Avila at the time. There was something disturbing in St. Teresa's tone, something harsh about it, and while I loved her use of language I couldn't really get into her writing. Then again, perhaps it was just a hard time for me and I wasn't able to con- centrate in general. I couldn't get beyond St. Teresa's account of her childhood with her brother Rodrigo. "We were astonished," the saint wrote, "that pain and bliss will last for ever; and very often we would discuss this saying. We took great pleasure in repeating over and over again: 'Forever, forever and ever.'"

The sea has always reminded me of infinity, and I'd sit on the porch, look out at the water, and read that over and over. I thought of little Teresa and Rodrigo sitting together, maybe holding hands, maybe looking seriously into each other's dark Spanish eyes, repeating over and over: *"Por siempre, por siempre y siempre . . ."* In the infinite quietude of a sky without lights or disturbance I would sit and pray, "forever, forever and ever. . . ."

I was afraid of ending something. I was afraid of drifting off into an unknown direction without knowing where I was going or why, just meandering off into something frightening until I gave up and ceased to exist. I was scared of starting something new alone. I was thinking a lot of things. I had been drawn to paganism in order to touch something beyond myself, but by this point I already had realized that I needed *more*. One of the main reasons I had fallen away from paganism into my vaguely pagan but increasingly orthodox Christianity was the fact that it seemed to provide something less ephemeral, something that would last. The saints talked about "forevers" and "everlastings" and "eternals" and "unendings" a lot, and I wanted to touch that, but I was missing something.

I used to believe in reincarnation, like a lot of people my age seem to—something about it appealed to the logical, patterned, mathematical part of my brain that I most likely inherited from my mother and that I think I have spent my entire life attempting to drown in the more creative aspects of my personality. But beyond that it was also the eternity of it all, the unending circle. I would imagine a line moving around circularly forever, always repeating, the wheel of samsara falling always forward into the past—but something about this would make me sick, the whole constriction of it all, the confinement, the repetition, the stagnancy. I wouldn't get this sick feeling when reading about Teresa's "ever-lasting," and I didn't know why. I had been repulsed at first by what I considered the normal Christian view of the afterlife because of its simplistic A followed by B plainness, and what I saw as an unfair balance between act and reward. "It doesn't make sense to punish someone for all eternity for how they acted for eighty years," I and many others have said. Yet here I was being attracted to this Christian mystic for precisely the reason I felt drawn away from the Christian afterlife—which is to say a release from the mathematical model into the freedom of a relationship with the Unknowable God without end, though always advancing, always moving, two candles in the same flame pulling closer, then apart, sparkling and longing always for *more*, more knowledge, more love.

To put it in less poetic words, I was drawn to the dynamic eternity of the Christian writers. I had been told—and agreed along with everyone else—that Christianity's afterlife was stagnant, and I flew from stagnancy. I had been told—and agreed—that Christianity's afterlife was too simple, and I flew from simplicity. Yet the farther I fled from stagnancy and over-simplicity, I found myself more drawn to St. Teresa's ideas—wandering eternally through the interior castle. Maybe, I thought, maybe that is what we are looking for. Reading about it made me realize how much I had longed for it without even realizing it—I hadn't wanted an endless cycle but an ever-deepening reality. . . . I thought of nature, how I loved it for its forever-ness, how I loved the sky and the sea for its unending-ness. I sat on the beach looking out on the cold blue water, drawn to it, seeing in it my reflection, touching it, as it moved and tumbled forward past the horizon.

I was changing—that's all I could think about. My interests were changing. I had always been interested in politics, for instance—I would read and watch the news with my mom and debate fervently. I had always been angered by my friends when they told me that they couldn't stand politics because it made no *real* difference. They just don't know, I had said, but now I was beginning to agree with them. It was small, I realized, and didn't really matter—not in the true sense. Countries and empires and kings change; the sea doesn't seem to. I was changing; I was less sure of myself. I didn't know what I believed in, and I didn't want to talk about everything anymore. I didn't know what to talk about, to anyone, to any of my friends. I was on the verge of something, starting to "feel in the rush of passing the stillness of the eternal," as I read Abraham Joshua Heschel write once. I was reading more, too, reading other people's ideas. To some extent I had always seen reading books on spirituality to be a hindrance to my own ideas, my own self—but I was quickly finding that I needed some roots if I ever wanted my relationship with the Divine to blossom.

The entire process was a matter of moving on from "me" to something more substantial. Current events, I had found, were ephemeral—and so was I. I recognized that I did not have all the answers; I was starting to realize that the world has existed longer than I have, and that it will exist long after my body has gone into the earth—I had to tap into something more than just myself. To some extent I have always had to do that—I remember one day in eighth grade outside on my deck during that beautiful spring that resurrected my jaded heart. The trees were lush and verdant, and I recall it had recently rained, dew hovering over the grass and flowers. I remember talking, then, to my gods, looking at the sky, which was shrouded in mist. I longed, I *ached*—I needed that sense of reality outside of myself. I talked to whatever goddess I hoped was listening, and protested—"I want to follow you," I whispered, out loud, "but I have no one to guide me, nothing, just myself; I am lost. I will never have the ability which I know the wise women who follow you do—until I find something or someone else. . . ." I knew that as long as I just stayed the way I was, I could never reach this power that I knew—somehow I knew—existed. I closed my eyes, listened to the whistling of the birds, and for a moment doubt came over me—was I talking to nothingness, to atmosphere? What was this delusion that had so suddenly possessed me?—I opened my eyes and, though it may have been an illusion, it seemed the mists had parted. I took this as a sign, then, for some reason, that change would come, that I would be led outside of just "me," be led to something pure, unending, eternal.

I was thinking all of this, too much of this, maybe, on Block Island, and I felt alone. On paper, change sounded beautiful, eternal change, eternal relationship with God, and it was what I had been longing for. It was what, it seemed, we all have been longing for. Countless times I have heard spiritually minded people my age talk about heaven—"Then what?" they ask: We die, and then what? Stagnancy can't be an option; it has to go on forever, changing, growing forever. (I later found the term *epektasis*, used by the church fathers, which outlines this idea perfectly—we eternally grow in our relationship to God, who can never be known essentially, from "glory to glory," infinitely.) I believed this, but change in reality was harder for me—my relationships changing, my beliefs changing, my entire self changing. I felt as if I was losing who I was, standing at the edge of a huge chasm, hair on end, letting myself dangle over the "abyss of divine infinitude."

I found my balance sometime later—"thus the soul, slipping at every point from what cannot be grasped, becomes dizzy and perplexed and returns once again to what is connatural to it," St. Gregory of Nyssa wrote—and everything started to make a little more sense. Looking back on it I can see it more clearly—my uncertainly, my shock and discomfort, was a necessary point in my movement towards the unknown and unending. I, like so many others, had said that I longed for the eternal, but was unwilling to let go of my former self, was unwilling to let go of the ever-changing present to move on toward the Truth. I was forced head-on into the real-life application of my pretty ideas, something I had never faced in all of my different beliefs, varying religions, and persistent tailoring of ancient ideas to my own self. The eternal is not only something that continues on for a straight line in the future but also is the ever-existent "other" that separates us from the divine reality. We all long for that, and when it comes, it shocks us with its demand that we let go of ourselves.

At my bat mitzvah, my rabbi had talked about the Temple in Jerusalem, about the separate—holy—Temple, the House of God that was a place of peace for all generations, even when the rest of reality was in shambles. It was this concept—which rang in my atheist ears on the day I became a daughter of the commandments—that drew me to the Eucharist, the divine presence in the world, the infinite in the finite, just as Christ was God in man. I recognized that even when I believed in reincarnation, in other planes, in relativism, what I was really searching for was the moment outside of time in which everything has its source, "something more, something beyond." A girl I know once described it to me, attempting to explain her thirst for something more than what she had experienced in her eclectic paganism—and I was searching for the realization of that moment in the here, now—the Incarnation, the eternal moment having taken on time and sanctified it. And so we must always align ourselves with this moment—we change, God doesn't. Our relationship with God deepens, but He is beyond all movement. People I know reject a God in time. A temporal God is too comprehensible, too flat. Meditation, speculation into other lives, divination—it's all about tapping into the eternal.

So the sea for me is a reflection of eternity, of not just a straight line going out infinitely, but a body of unspeakable depth and unutterable beauty. I haven't been to Block Island since, and wonder whether if I go back there I will see what I saw then. I wonder if it was my perception that saw it, or if the water truly did talk to me that summer. It's better not to go back to those moments outside of time, which shake us and toss us into new life as new creatures. They don't come back, but there shall be others, all part of the same eternal moment—"all things pass," wrote St. Teresa; "God never changes."

SEVEN
Searching for Ourselves

"We can never see the state of our soul in all
its nakedness . . . without the special grace and
help of God, because the interior of our soul
is always hidden from us by our self-love,
prejudices, passions, worldly cares, delusions."

—St. Innocent of Alaska, *Indication of
the Way into the Kingdom of Heaven*

At the end of my junior year, I was helping some people in my grade—some of them friends, some just acquaintances—study for finals as we sat outside at the stone tables in front of the Student Center. History—after English—is my area of expertise, so a few people had asked me to explain some concepts to them; I believe we were discussing the modern world. At one point I mentioned, somewhat jokingly, that I dislike most history from the Enlightenment to the present day, and one girl, Jess, asked me why—and this soon became a discussion of philosophy.

"I dislike all philosophies centered on the self," I said, almost in passing.

"Why shouldn't we think about the self?"

"Because it doesn't make you happy," I said nonchalantly, and was surprised by her response—silence, almost shocked.

"That's true," she said after a while.

"Thinking about the self too much always makes you unhappy," I repeated.

This, though I didn't mention it then, is from personal experience. So much of my life was spent "searching" for myself, finding myself, discovering "who I am." That used to bother me, and I used to think about it a lot. I wanted a genuine sense of self—not just attributes to list—and I wanted to somehow accept that, have that somehow be enough. My friend Melissa and I gave psychoanalyses of each other once, and I remember relishing everything she could say about me, feeding off it, needing to know how she saw me, how others saw me, *who I was*. I think that's really why I used to write—I knew that my subconscious would float to the surface somehow and maybe give me some clues.

This might also be why I first started getting so interested in religion. To some extent I was inexplicably drawn to it, but it also was this seeking, not only for God, but for myself. *Me*. I wanted to be loved for who I was and I wanted to know why. Behind every selfless act I did—buying things for people, writing letters to people, helping people with homework, listening to friends—was a sort of underlying selfishness, a sort of unspoken, "but why can't you love me for who *I* am? And *who am I?*"

Above all, I think, I wanted to be told that I was special. It sounds corny, but that was always there; that was always the force behind everything. No matter how much someone loved me or told me they loved me, it wasn't enough; I was always empty, and I attributed my emptiness to the fact that no one valued me as a human being. Always, always, there was the obsession—as my friend Lynn put it—"the need to find someone who loves as passionately as you do," who has the full force of emotions that you have, directed towards *you*, so that for once you are the god of their idolatry . . . so that *you* are cherished, treasured, loved. I myself would obsess over people; I am wired for worship. I would find people to love with all my being, but selfishly, always wishing they

67

would love me back, always wondering why no one cared about me the way I cared about them.

I wasn't alone in this; I have many friends now who do the same thing, who need reassurance, always, that they are loved. Now I am seeing the other side of my former life: My friends always had to assure me that they cared, and sometimes got frustrated when I did not believe them. Now I feel the same way with my friends who constantly ask me, "Am I annoying?" "Do you really like me?" "Am I special?" This is distressing, and impossible to cure with logic.

I mention some of this as Jess and I talk philosophically— as the others look at us with vague bewilderment. I lit a spark somewhere, hit a switch, when I spoke those words—I know because I have always known, on some level, that it was true, and Jess knew it too. We talked about sacrifice and asceticism and crosses, and happiness and love and true life. She agreed with most everything I said, as if it were obvious. As always when I talk to my friends about "deep things," I am surprised how much common ground there is. I left God out of most of my arguments, left out the more complex theology I study, but talked purely as someone who believes in joy, and believes that it has very little to do with self-value.

"The self is so small," I said at one point, and started thinking about it.

I don't remember exactly when "the self" as the definite object of my quest became irrelevant to me. I don't know who I am, really, and I don't always feel that others love me when they say they do—I'm still a bit paranoid when it comes to the people I love. But it doesn't really matter that much to me now; I have stopped thinking about myself so much. As Fr. Aidan Nichols noted in his *Epiphany: A Theological Introduction to Catholicism*: "I become aware that I am not so much an 'I' looking for a divine 'Thou' as a 'thou' engaged by the divine 'I.'" I have come to recognize that I am not the focal point of existence; I exist only in relation to One who is beyond me. All existence comes from elsewhere.

Self-esteem is not the same thing as self-love, I suppose. I never treated myself well, I never thought much of myself, but in general throughout my life I was always obsessed with myself. I guess I still don't always treat myself very well, but increasingly I've found that I'm happiest when I almost forget that I exist, and concern myself with more important things. Ironically, it is when I forget about myself that I start to truly find out who I am; when I focus on others my place in the world, brought down from the exalted throne I imagined for it, becomes clearer. I always wanted to be told that I was special—I always wanted a reason to value myself. But when the perfect comes, the imperfect disappears, and when I started valuing what was outside myself, I found, in that, my value. Whoever loses his life will save it.

Most popular books on spirituality are basically self-help books—how can a religion help *me*? Religion or, more appropriately, "spirituality," is viewed as a sort of fix that humanity needs, a drug. It is not about finding Truth, about submitting the self to something greater—it is about the gratification of the self. Interestingly, though, this is paired with the complete opposite. Invariably I hear two things from people my age—they either want the self valued above all things or completely obliterated. "Deny yourself and take up your cross and follow me" is seen as unduly harsh—the process should be one of self-actualization, not self-denial, I am told. But on the other hand, many teens find answers in religions and philosophies where the self is, ultimately, negated (as in popular strands of pseudo-Buddhism), or assumed into a greater Being. And I suppose that's the other side of the coin for a people obsessed with who they are—the realization that the question only leads to unhappiness, and finally, futility and despair. And this realization leads to the quest for the death of the self. "I don't want to believe in something where we keep on living after we die," I've heard.

I wanted that too. I could deal with the idea of eternal life, but only in the context of the obliteration of self-consciousness. I was sick of myself, even as I obsessed over who I was, tried to think of ways that I could value myself more. I was infatuated with the idea of self-esteem, but believed in a philosophy of self-negation. Was I that torn? Looking back, I guess I must have been.

What would I have said if someone had talked to me then, someone who believes what I do now? I'm not sure.

I do not know if I would have responded—and now, I wonder how far I should go with people who remind me of my former self; I have to remember not to sound preachy. I have what makes me complete, or, more accurately, is my complete source of joy, but I do not think I can just explain it to people—you can't do that. But my own person has become bound with who God is—I can't have a deep conversation or write anything of value without reference to Him. There is no Marjorie that I center my life on anymore; at least not consciously. When I talk about chemistry homework, or discuss teachers or movies or music, or talk about friends, I am fine, but any time the exchange goes a little deeper, it has everything to do with Him for me. The first person starts to fade away as you go down.

Jess doesn't seem to mind, anyway. In the student center—suddenly her face lights up, and she says, "Marjorie! Oh!"

I tilt my head. "Yes?"

She's distracted for a second, but then turns around and points at me. I raise my eyebrows and wait for her to go on. She moves some little curls out of her face, and starts.

"I got this book, and it's, like, all of what we talked about. I really like it."

I ask for the name of the author, wondering what kind of self-help book this could be, and her response ("Fulton . . . Fulton something?") makes me smile, as

I know that Bishop Sheen will answer everything for her better than I could.

For a moment I wonder what would happen if everyone around me were to read something like Bishop Fulton Sheen instead of the books usually prescribed for affirming self-worth, instead of books that do nothing but confuse us into thinking that we can exist in and of ourselves, and not in relation to others and to God. The fact that Jess—pretty, rich, as much into makeup and boys as most teenage girls—would say "I really like it" about one of the, well, *Marjorie books*, as my friends would probably call them, gave me a bit of hope.

I wander through my world of icons, darkness and candles, memories and bittersweet faith, carrying my own cross, and it's sometimes hard for me to remember who I used to be, who I am now. The upper-case letter "I" looks ugly—thin and rigid—to me, and the fact that I still don't know who I am upsets me sometimes. I forget that what I believe isn't here for me. All my searching for self met its end in the realization that none of it matters, that I can only really find myself in giving myself up, that everyone will realize who I am once I've become irrelevant to myself. I relish the paradox, but sometimes it won't translate into reality, and sometimes I'm pulled down with my friends into the abyss of that perpetual question— "Who am I?"

Sometimes I end up in the right place. By my nightstand sits an icon of Christ as the Divine Wisdom, an icon that

I got in New York not so long ago. The colors are striking, forceful. His steady hand, blessing, entices the eye to travel up further to His illuminated face—all gold and brown and white. The eyes make me stop dead in my tracks. A red circle, lines and Greek letters surround his head, all pushing down into the eyes, those eyes, which actually are rather small, though glowing.

"Who do you say that I am?" they seem to ask me, just as they asked the apostles. This is about Him, I see. This is not about me.

I can't answer like Peter, though I know his response by heart. I sit silent like the rest of them, staring, humbled.

"Who do you say that I am?"

I want to say, "Lord, I don't know, but I know that I love You!"

And His little mouth vaguely smiles, and pushes off light toward me.

"And you don't know who you are," I seem to hear, "but you know that I love you."

It doesn't matter, says the thought, and I put the icon away.

EIGHT
Craving for Community

"Let us love one another, so that with

one mind we may confess . . ."

—from the *Divine Liturgy of St. John Chrysostom*

Rio was five years older than I, and I was a freshman. At the time that kind of gap between us seemed enormous, though I wouldn't have settled for anything less. I needed guidance at the time—a teacher, an older sister, anything. She was so much larger than life to me—Sagrario Quisqueya Feliz—with her stone-black eyes and her expressionless face, and for a long time I worshiped her.

I don't use that word figuratively. I'm a religious person by temperament, I think, and my natural orientation is always toward worship. Before I believed in God—or at least in a God I was comfortable worshiping—adulation sort of bubbled up within me and directed itself toward people, human beings of flesh and blood and faults and limitations. Rio was my most powerful and certainly my most beautiful idol.

She called me *"bebé"*—I picked up a lot of Spanish from her and her friends—and told me that I was special. She more than almost anyone that I have ever met appreciated my writing, looked forward to reading things I would write—and I was always ready to write things for her— and enjoyed saying "wow" repeatedly after she read them. She was spiritual, though I wouldn't say religious, and I tried desperately to adopt her beliefs, her exotic spirituality, her gods and goddesses, her Mother of the Ocean whose Children Are the Fish.

I met her through Daphne Rubin-Vega, the original Mimi in *Rent* and as amazing a human being as she is an artist. For over a year, probably, my life, heart, and mind arranged itself in a circle around the sun of Daphne. My closest friends were fans of hers, most of my social life involved going to her concerts, and most of my thoughts went either to her or to those of us who were connected through her. She would sing the same songs—break down the walls with her voice—and tell the same lame stories, and we would all laugh affectionately.

I think I must have known, then, that the problem was that I needed a community. I smiled broadly whenever Rio or the others would refer to our group as "The Posse," and whenever Daphne came over to us after shows, looked at us with love and even, perhaps, a little gratitude, I felt that, I *knew* that what I wanted was somewhere to belong, somewhere I could feel accepted— this sounds clichéd, I know, but everyone knows that it is true.

I was starting a new school and I didn't really fit in yet. I would sit alone at lunch, or at the same table with people with whom I would not converse, and I sat, silent, throughout most of my classes. With strangers, I am very shy, and more than a little paranoid. Due on the whole to my social experiences at the public school in my town, I often find it hard to believe that others want to talk to me, or hear what I have to say, or be around me. By the end of the year I was loud enough, and by the next school year I had friends enough, but at this point, all I had was the group of people I knew from online and Daphne's concerts—most of them lived in New York City (about forty-five minutes away from me), though some lived in Pennsylvania, Florida, California. Most all of them were older than I was.

Eventually, of course, the house of cards folded and my heart broke. It was stupid how it happened, at first so suddenly, and then gradually. I wanted so dearly to be part of a group that I found it hard to refuse anyone anything—I just wanted to be accepted. That's when I made my mistake, and I lost it all somehow: One friend coaxed me into sharing some information I had promised Rio I wouldn't share, and it became impossible to go back: The breach was there. Eventually the scars faded, but things were never the same. It's just a blurry story inscribed on the regretful walls of my memory. The intense connection with these people and the loss that followed a stupid mistake—the worshiping of idols and their destruction—it's all there in me, floating through the library of the mind.

I believe in other things now, but I still believe that humans need love and community. Maybe it's just because we're pack animals, but we can't live, we can't sleep at night without knowing that other people love us, that other people are there for us, and hopefully even will live or die for us.

It seems like the past year for me has been a gradual process of phasing myself off of everything in my life that was a fake, pretend version of something that I needed, and learning to accustom myself to the real thing, something that isn't always easy and isn't always as gratifying or as safe as the old thing. It's like taking off the training wheels and learning to ride a bike. I can't say that I still don't fall—but I am happy about it. My ideas about community, relationships, people, and love are no different. I used to surround myself with love that couldn't really hurt me, with people who couldn't be completely real to me, until those people became real and I ended up hurt. I spend a lot less time on-line now—though I still spend way too much, arguing politics and religion on messageboards—and the people with whom I talk on-line aren't my closest friends, though there are many whom I love dearly. That means that I have to face real people with real imperfections when I want to see those who are close to me; it means that I have to take more risks, and I have to stop living in a world that doesn't exist. This wasn't something that just came to me—I came to it, because I knew I had to.

After the sand castle of my system of friends fell apart as tenth grade began, I immersed myself in something I found increasingly difficult to ignore—religion. I had lost most of what was truly dear to me, and during that period of loss I began to become even more interested in mythology, in spirituality, in the great traditions of all the world's religions. And I found myself drawn above all else, without understanding why, to the story of Jesus.

From the very beginning, even in my most neo-pagan, neo-Gnostic stage, the Gospel of John was my favorite of the four Gospels, especially for its emphasis on love. Not only love as an abstract force of good, but love as a reality, like flesh or bread or a human being, that could literally bind together all the people in the world. "A new commandment I give to you," Jesus repeatedly insisted, "that you love one another; as I have loved you, that you also love one another. By this all will know that you are My disciples, if you have love for one another."

"As I have loved you . . ." For so long I had confused love with affection, with infatuation. I began, when I read the Gospel of John, to see a new definition—Jesus' love demanded blood. It wasn't simply comforting, it was a promise and a surrender, complete giving without the single thought of repayment. This was completely foreign to me, I who had cried for so many hours for the sole reason that I loved Rio—and everyone else—more than, I believed, they could ever love me back. I had been loving for the sole reason that I needed to love.

It's amazing how things can be transformed in so little time. The words "Jesus loves me" would only have aroused anger or mockery in me a year ago, and at the very least I would have regarded the statement with the condescending air of one who knew that it was a silly and offensive, if well-intentioned, remark. I would have thought that it was a symptom of the dumbed-down religion Christianity had become. Now, of course, after having read the New Testament in full, after having read much more complicated theology than I had read then, after having studied the faith's history and origins much more thoroughly, I realize that the simple phrase is, in the end, all that ever needs to be said. Christianity in its most complex form is nothing more than a growth from the firm conviction that, indeed, Jesus does love me, and that Jesus' love can change everything.

I long for people who can understand me, who can help me, guide me, touch me, pierce my heart the way that it seemed that Rio and the rest of the "posse" did. And some days it gets hard, sometimes I want what I had then, security and affection and the sort of young girl's passion reserved only for first loves and replacement goddesses. On the worst of days I realize that I don't have that sort of passion when it comes to my friends now— only people, only real people, who sometimes annoy me, to whom it's harder to talk because there's more of a risk, people with whom I have to actually create friendships.

But I know that this is where I have to be right now, and I know why. I know that I can't expect love to work like a toy or a high, that love is work, and a promise, and self-sacrifice, as much as it is wonderful. I believe that humans have been created to experience love in its greatest reality, and that doesn't mean just fake worship, even of the most beautiful of people, the most intriguing, the most worthy of admiration.

It's not possible to exaggerate the number people I have met who create false communities for themselves, who trust in an artificial kind of love, especially the kind that an Internet community can ensure. Like every inherently good thing, the computer can be as evil as it is good, and can hinder as much as it can help. The intoxicating thrill of being able to choose friends from millions of people while still retaining a perpetual veil of anonymity and security is enough to destroy more lonely little girls than me as I was in ninth grade. But it's not just the Internet—people don't need that excuse. I used to say, when I was first getting into religion, that reality is fragile, and that might well be true, but I would say even more than that now that reality is hard. The need to be in a group, the need to belong, the need to be loved, is only one side of the coin—the other is the fact that it's not easy, that people aren't just abstract concepts but flesh and bone and you can't play with them. They have needs and insecurities, and getting into their world is dangerous. It requires giving up one's self, not hoarding their love to yourself.

So much has changed since ninth grade—enter Jesus, exit my old friends. And Rio? How I loved her then—so passionately. It would have seemed blasphemy to think, then, that life would go on without her being there, that I would find other senses of being loved, of being part of something. And yet, here I am, surrounded by the community of my flesh and blood friends, and the community of faith and love that I find over and over again in the Church. It is so different, at times harder, but it is better for me. I moved from sickness to health.

Rio's dark curls surrounding her softly beautiful face are still enough to bring me to tears. I'm more comfortable with her now, when I see her, because it's not like before—I'm not so petrified. But there's still something in me that wants to go back to the way it was, when she was everything to me, when a word from her could fill my world with light or shatter it to pieces.

It all floods back for a moment, the deep black of her eyes competing with the fire of new faith, and I smile back at her. I love her, I tell myself, but it's never going to be the same again.

NINE
Moving From Rights to Obligations

"And again we offer unto Thee this reasonable service,

for the whole world . . . and for all mankind."

—from the *Divine Liturgy of St. John Chrysostom*

There is a mosaic in the thirteenth-century church of St. Tommaso in Formis, Rome, which I never would have dated to the Middle Ages. Christ is enthroned—regal and serene. This much is familiar, especially in Eastern iconography. He holds out His hands in a symmetrical pose, peacefully and calmly, yet the two figures He touches are caught unawares, unbalanced, startled. He is holding on to the arms of two slaves, both wearing nothing but simple cloth garments from the waist to the knees. Both have feet in chains. The one on Christ's right carries a cross, and looks up, shocked. The slave on Christ's left looks down at his hands, his mouth agape, as if he had never before seen his own body. He is black. Christ looks neither to the left nor right, but stares ahead, crowned in majesty, haloed with light.

I first stumbled upon this mosaic in The *Oxford Illustrated History of Christianity* and was fascinated. I researched it a bit and found that it is a depiction of the seal of the Order of the Holy Trinity and the Captives, a Catholic order whose main task was to free slaves. Somewhere in my mind notions of equality and justice registered—the dogma of my earlier years and the great concern of my present. As long as I can remember I have been obsessed with fairness, with all things working out justly. A story my mother likes to tell is of me at one and a half assuring her that I would not get chicken pox a second time as this would simply not be fair. On the other hand, I was always baffled by questions as to whether I would rather be fair or right—as the question in the personality test model is put. In my mind these have always been equated instead of opposed. Justice is truth, truth is justice: That was all I knew and all I needed to know.

Before I became Christian, my views as to religion and justice were quite different than they are today. I had always assumed that Christianity was a religion of inherent inequality. The Christian faith, I was taught, was other-worldly minded and not generally concerned with the well-being of others despite its lip-service to charity. Yet I wasn't just anti-Christian—I had always associated faith itself with inequality. Within my own religious context, while I had been taught to appreciate the Jewish tradition of social justice (*tikkun olam*), I had also always been taught by my Hebrew school teachers and others to understand the biblical concept of a "chosen people" as irrational and elitist. We were Reform Jews—we didn't believe in that or anything like it. The Orthodox Jews with their talk of a messiah, strange rituals, and archaic customs could believe that they were chosen, but that was not our concern. It seemed to me, then, as a child, that the farther I moved away from religiosity the closer I got to fairness; religion was divisive by definition, whereas equality is an all-embracing concept. As I grew older I accepted the common line that religion exists primarily as a tool to subjugate the masses, to promote injustice and inequities under the general banner of heaven and the life to come.

Many of my opinions came through contact with others. Intelligent teenagers, of course, believe that God is a political ploy and a psychological delusion. Religion, they believe, plays on the basest of human instincts, justifying hatred and militant behavior and prejudice. In a discussion in class this year of what many view as President Bush's narrow world-view of black and white, infidels and crusaders, sinners and saints, one of my peers identified this as the natural extension of the president's religiosity: "It's all this fundamentalism. We need an atheist as a president." Others laughed or nodded. I didn't. I don't laugh at those kind of jokes anymore, which might be the reason that many people have decided I must be a right-wing conservative despite the fact that I have been liberal all my life, and still am except on a few issues.

This was not an isolated incident by any means. One of the most contentious debates I have had with my older sister, Rachel—with whom I am very close—was at Thanksgiving at our aunt and uncle's house a few years ago. Someone mentioned something in the paper about religion; she contested that the more religious a nation or a person was, the more prejudiced, the more oppressive. I disagreed, though at the time I was not religious in the way I am now, and soon we were yelling, she was crying, and my mom was trying to calm us down so that the other members of our family wouldn't be disturbed by our clash. I spent the rest of the day sulking, as Rachel and my mother left the house—to get away from me, I assumed. It's hard to remember how we even got into such a passionate argument over something that should be remote, not personal, but I have discovered this is a topic that inspires anger at its fundamental core.

The mosaic of the impartial Jesus for me symbolizes everything that is wrong with my former mindset. I didn't know what justice was when I worshiped it. In the broad terms of ideology it meant that everyone had the same intrinsic worth, everyone should be able to do what he or she wanted. More specifically I really saw it as everyone being "the same" deep down. I didn't, however, have a real consistent philosophy behind it all—I just knew that my heart burned for "the better part"—for something beyond what we had. I knew that what I saw in the world was simply not good enough. I saw the world infected with man-made evils, and, without believing in anything beyond the world I saw, I fell into frustration and despair. I wanted so much to make the world perfect! I share that with many people my age—the frustration, the anger over the world, sick and fallen as it is. I just did not know how to go about fixing it.

I knew what I in particular had to do: support this bill or write to my senator about this program in order to promote equality for women, blacks, Hispanics, immigrants, gays, etc. But behind that, not much. Somewhere in me, even if I wasn't prepared to recognize it, my Hebrew school education of *tzedakah* and *mitzvot* (charity and good deeds) perhaps prevented me from accepting more modern ideas of justice and equality. I never was too interested in the "natural rights" ideology of the Enlightenment; it seemed then and now to be rather bland and half-hearted to me. Neither could I accept my mother's discussions of an economically ideal society where the inequities of one affect the inequities of all. That was all too cold and too mathematical to provoke such a passion inside me for liberty, equality, and fraternity. It was a passion, an obsession, at times even to the extent of idolatry. We had never talked this way—in terms of statistical models—in Hebrew school. It had always been a matter of what God asked us to do, what we knew we had to do. It wasn't a scientific system; it was a command and an obedience.

The mosaic, a simple seal of a religious order, tells me more than I ever could have believed then—God frees the captives, and doesn't look to the left or to the right. It reminds me of the statues of Blindfolded Justice—scales in her left hand, sword in her left, carved in the smooth coolness of neo-classical sculpture—how the Ruler of All looks straight ahead with His unmoving forwardness; yet unlike Justice, His arms are outstretched, unloosing bonds.

Simone Weil, one of my favorite philosophers, wrote that the concept of "rights" was misguided—one could not imagine St. Francis of Assisi talking about rights. I agree with her—I have come to believe in obligations instead. It is a matter of emphasis, of perception, but it makes all the difference. Since I have switched over from doubt to faith, while I do not always live up to my ideals, I have felt for the first time in my life a real sense of duty, of responsibility. For the first time, I have seen my life as a matter of what I am charged to do—not what others are bound to do for me.

Sophocles' Antigone stood for the "immortal, unrecorded laws of God" that compelled her to bury her brother, not for her brother's entitlement to burial. How beautiful Antigone was to me when I read the play in ninth grade—how strong was this rebellious daughter of Oedipus! She did not exist for herself. I knew then, that I was drawn to that—a life lived for others, a life of self-sacrifice. It was crazy and idealistic, and Antigone died for it, but I knew, then, that I could not live with anything less. This is justice—the work of God on earth—self-sacrifice, self-emptying, losing yourself in love for man, made in the image of God, of the race that God Himself became incarnate. Sameness and equality are terms that have gradually lost their relevancy for me—what is relevant is my duty to save all that I can, as all is made by God, who is infinitely good.

Religion—what does that word even mean? For me, it doesn't have much to do with justice, but God the Father has a lot to do with it, as does Christ. I do not think that religion necessarily fosters justice, and perhaps my peers are right that religion can justify cruelty. I don't have any interest in arguing about the Crusades or the Inquisition or the satanic bonfires of Salem, Massachusetts, or even worse, Christian acts of inequity today, such as harassment of homosexuals or women. This is always what I encounter when talking to people about religion, and this is what my sister was repelled by when we discussed it. It wasn't the religion, but the fact, as she perceived it, that religious people had done evil. And that is true; evil is sown in us, all of us, even those who have checked into the hospital of the Christian Church. I wish I could point fingers of blame like I used to, at certain groups of people, at certain ideas, at prejudices, at concentrations of power. But now there is a higher calling, not to an ideology, but to justice—God's justice. Words like "religion" confuse things, but God makes everything clear. We want justice because it is His will, and He is waiting for us to act. He looks forward, neither to the right nor to the left, and holds out our hands so that we may begin unloosing chains.

TEN

Whoever Would Have Life Must Lose It

"Unless we go through this fire that consumes the decaying passions of our nature, we shall not see the fire transformed into light: . . . in our fallen state burning precedes enlightenment. Let us, therefore, bless God for this consuming fire."

—Archimandrite Sophrony, *His Life is Mine*

Maybe it's because it's the middle of the day and the light can't help pouring into the windows in fluid showers of sun, but I realize, sitting at the lunch table, that the three friends sitting with me are in the exact positions of the figures in Andrei Rublev's celebrated icon of the Old Testament Trinity. I bought the Tarkovsky film *Andrei Rublev* the other day, so perhaps that's why this occurs to me, but after I see it, it becomes clear, tangible—I can almost taste it.

The Rublev icon shows three angels sitting around a table, each one representing one of the three Persons of the Holy Trinity—Father, Son, and Holy Spirit—based on a narrative in Genesis where three angels visit Abraham. The plural morphs into singular and back throughout the passage: On one hand Abraham is talking to "the LORD," and on the other hand three separate beings are in front of him. The icon is considered to be the greatest of all Russian icons, and perhaps even the greatest icon of all time.

On the far left of my real-life icon, Laura is sitting in the position that is often understood to be that of God the Father. She's telling something to the others—something that happened, maybe, something funny anyway—and instead of holding out her hand in blessing to the others as with the Rublev icon, she's holding both hands out in gestures, moving, explaining, illustrating. She's smiling, and that reassures me as my eyes move to the far right, where Jenny with her illuminated smile is sitting in the place of the Spirit. Her bright red curls are crowned with gold in the light, and I can almost imagine in them the fiery tongues of the first Pentecost. Her face—as in the icon—is turned toward the left, bowed a little, listening, humming in silence. In the middle of the scene is the seat of Christ which is filled by—of course—my beloved Christine. Her hands, like in the original, point in front of her gently—not to the Eucharistic gifts, as we have none—but seemingly to me. The whole picture points toward sacrifice.

It was hard, at first, for me to accept the concept of Christian asceticism. I associated it with medieval monks starving themselves and wearing hair shirts. On a better day, the words at least reminded me of the monks in *Monty Python and the Holy Grail* singing a hymn punctuated by hitting one's self on the head with a board. It took me a long time to understand true *askesis* as a means of purification, healing, through the power of the Cross— the stumbling block and foolishness of every generation. It was certainly a stumbling block and foolishness to me, anyway. I took for granted what I had always been taught—that everyone is naturally good, that in this world we have certain rights to happiness that should not be denied. Most of my peers, I think, would agree with those statements. Yet I have found that these principles just do not stand up to scrutiny. Yes, we were created to be good. Yes, we have been created to be happy. But whoever would have life must lose it.

Even now, I try to ignore the gesture of the lunchtime icon towards self-sacrifice—so hard, when I truly realize its implications—and try to focus on the three figures without it. I look at them and smile, hoping for a moment that they won't see me, so that I can simply watch them with love. Each of them stands out beautifully, and draws me in completely. The fifteenth-century icon lifts my heart up to God, but this twenty-first century one delights in the beauty of the world made by His hands, and the people therein. I look at the three people, united by the one simple truth of love haloing around them, and think. And they all lead me back again to sacrifice.

Christine is one of the most peculiar people I have ever met. She has the strange, idiosyncratic charity of the saints—a sort of insane beauty. She exudes kindness; she breathes it. She sings with an otherworldly brilliance, and her eyes are blue crystal. As I began to read the Scriptures—*really* read the Scriptures—the words began to come to me almost involuntarily, at random points, moving from my heart to my mind constantly. Over and over again Christine would illumine for me some dark passage of the Gospels that I had not understood before, or simply a truth I did not truly believe: "Love one another, as I have loved you. . . ."

If Christine was for me a key to the Gospel of John, Jenny has been to me all the psalms—the bright, passionate understanding of God's presence. All the virtues of goodness, sweetness, are made manifest in her, hidden somewhere in those dimples, or freckles, or dark green eyes. She sits where the Spirit sits, and has always seemed the least distant, has always seemed the most accessible of all of them.

Laura fits in more with the five books of Moses—books that have always been very comforting and close to me, and this is very appropriate for her—bringing us all back to the Genesis setting of the icon. Harder to grasp than the other two, she is the one I have known for the shortest time (and this, I suppose, makes sense in this portrait, considering that I accepted the two figures of the Trinity she does not represent before I accepted the Father). Light covering darkness, I let her explain for herself, as she sits stuck forever in a perfect moment, sitting around a table with two friends.

The perfection of this whole picture is that I have to be willing to realize that I have to give it up. All the beauty of the world—and there can be no more beauty in the world than in my friends—is not worth a soul, even one chained down by passions and a tendency toward sin and death. I do not think many people I know believe this. We're told to believe in ourselves; we're told that we have entitlements. But rights are only effectual in a round-about way—there are obligations that come before them.

Two of the above-mentioned friends lost something this year, and both times I helped by looking for it for them. Christine lost her wallet one day, and Jenny lost a bracelet. While looking both times, noticing their very obvious distress—alarming distress—there was a temptation to self-righteously think to myself of the words of the Gospels: "Lay not up for yourselves treasures upon earth, where moth and rust doth corrupt, and where thieves break through and steal: but lay up for yourselves treasures in heaven . . . for where your treasure is, there will your heart be also." Yet I knew that this was misguided, even then. The irony, of course, is that the treasure that I prefer so often to God is not food, is not clothes, or jewelry—but my friends. This sounds like a rather bland statement at first, but I take it to be literally true: I love my friends too much.

I worship people; that is my weakness. I'm not a materialistic person, so giving up possessions has always been easy for me. I always liked the story of the rich man whom Jesus asked to give up everything so that he would follow Him; for me this would be simple. Yet it's not a matter of what is effortless. I am infatuated with people; I expect them to give more to me than they can. I so need human connection, community, touch, that these things have become somewhat of an idol for me—I expect those I love to be more than human. I have to give them up, give up my passionate affection towards them, in order to love them as concrete human beings, to love them for who they are, not for what they are not.

The spirit of Christian asceticism, I had to admit while watching my friends shine in the afternoon sun, is not a spirit of bondage but of freedom. My friends store up for themselves treasures on earth, maybe, but I do that too. We've all been taught to do this, and, for a fallen world, it is natural to do. But the finite cannot satisfy us. It leads only to emptiness. All our sadnesses, all our little failures— they all depend on our reliance on something that is not God, in putting trust in princes and sons of men.

I fast from food because I want to be free from my stomach, from my unnatural desires, from everything that doesn't bring me closer to the will of God. We are created as "hungry beings," prepared for a feast, but to live to eat is to become slaves to food. The same can be applied to almost any aspect of our lives—the danger of indulgence. We are almost encouraged by our elders to be animals, to satisfy any instinct that we have at any time. We are not treated as if we are expected to be responsible, and then many wonder why so many of us destroy ourselves in the same way. Yet even with this tendency toward self-indulgence, there is a sense that we all have that this is not enough. There is an emptiness that surrounds our gluttony, which leads to rejection of what does not satiate us. For me, it is simple. Nothing but the kingdom of heaven can completely satisfy me, can completely make me happy, not even the most beautiful people in the world.

Christine's hand points softly at me, at this body of death. I try to remember Paul's words—"present your bodies a living sacrifice, holy, acceptable to God. . . ." (Romans 12:1b). The vision of my friends becomes a little blurry as I think these words, and this is good because they are so hard to look at. I know that I have to leave, and pray. Even though it's a Friday, and a fast day, I've still eaten too much, and my soul and all my being seems pulled down into the hard weight of my stomach. I try to separate myself from it, but the light that had been so airy and soft just a moment ago is burning too harshly in my eyes.

"Lord Jesus Christ, have mercy upon me, a sinner," I whisper weakly, hoping this prayer will do something. I sit there, and think.

Christian love is inseparable from sacrifice. We try to separate it; we try to take Christ's social teachings and separate them from His spiritual ones. But they are all one and the same. Everything is about denying ourselves, taking up our cross and following Him—only there is joy instead of instant gratification.

This sounds so easy in theory, on paper, but the reality is hard. Be free, the Gospels urge us, and I want to apply this to my life—sometimes it slips from my grasp. Whatever is most precious to us, whatever gods we have been worshiping, we have to give up so that we can receive them as gifts, as grace, and not as our taproot of life. Humanity is in chains—but whoever loses his life for the Lord will save it.

I want to love my friends perfectly, I think, as I watch them start to move, as I watch them not as angels but as three teenage girls at the lunch table. Laura has finished the story, and Christine is laughing and fanning herself, a weird quirk of hers. Jenny is smiling brightly. The words of the Liturgy come to me as prayer: "Let us commit ourselves and each other and all our lives unto Christ our God." And when I give everything up, when I truly deny myself and take up my cross and follow Him, maybe I can love those that I already love in a truer manner, maybe I can love them as an icon of the love and sacrifice of the Holy Trinity.

I'm writing this, and I know that tomorrow I will hear Christine sing again. I know that her voice will have something of heaven in it, and I know that I will be moved. But the point, I know, is that it's not my friend that moves me, but all the miraculous gifts, all the incredible truth and beauty that the Father of All has given her, and to all those I love. I try to remember that, and try to pray, and try to commit myself and all my life unto Christ my God.

About Paraclete Press

Who We Are

Paraclete Press is an ecumenical publisher of books on Christian spirituality for people of all denominations and backgrounds.

We publish books that represent the wide spectrum of Christian belief and practice—Catholic, Orthodox, and Protestant.

We market our books primarily through booksellers; we are what is called a "trade" publisher, which means that we like it best when readers buy our books from booksellers, our partners in successfully reaching as wide an audience as possible.

We are uniquely positioned in the marketplace without connection to a large corporation or conglomerate and with informal relationships to many branches and denominations of faith, rather than a formal relationship to any single one. We focus on publishing a diversity of thoughts and perspectives—the fruit of our diversity as a company.

What We Are Doing

Paraclete Press is publishing books that show the diversity and depth of what it means to be Christian. We publish books that reflect the Christian experience across many cultures, time periods, and houses of worship.

We publish books about spiritual practice, history, ideas, customs, and rituals, and books that nourish the vibrant life of the church.

We have several different series of books within Paraclete Press, including the bestselling Living Library series of modernized classic texts, A Voice from the Monastery—giving voice to men and women monastics on what it means to live a spiritual life today, and Many Mansions—for exploring the riches of the world's religious traditions and discovering how other faiths inform Christian thought and practice.

Learn more about us at our website:
www.paracletepress.com, or call us toll-free at
1-800-451-5006.

If you liked *A Tiny Step Away from Deepest Faith*, you will also enjoy:

Mudhouse Sabbath

Lauren F. Winner,
author of *Girl Meets God*
144 pages, ISBN: 1-55725-344-7
$17.95 Hardcover

Despite her conversion from Orthodox Judaism to Christianity, Lauren Winner finds that her life is still shaped by the spiritual essences of Judaism—rich traditions and religious practices that she can't leave behind. In *Mudhouse Sabbath*, this compelling young writer illuminates eleven spiritual practices that can transform the way we view the world, and God. Whether discussing her own prayer life, the spirituality of candle-lighting, or the differences between the Jewish Sabbath and a Sunday spent at the "Mudhouse," her favorite coffee shop, Winner writes with appealing honesty and rare insight.

"Lauren Winner speaks the language of this generation. It is authentic, free, and bold."
    —Ben Young, co-author of *The Ten Commandments of Dating*

"At a time when we are so aware of the differences between Judaism and Christianity, Lauren Winner's book on what we can learn from each other is refreshingly welcome."
    —Rabbi Harold Kushner, author of
    When Bad Things Happen to Good People

"Lauren's writing is hospitable, as if you're sitting cross-legged in her crowded apartment, eating a slice of pizza and chatting about her insightful, educational, and warmly invasive reflections."
    —Mark Oestreicher, President and Publisher, *Youth Specialties*

"For all of us who can't get our spiritual lives in shape by shipping out to a monastery, Lauren Winner has given us *Mudhouse Sabbath*. She explores ways—simple, do-able ways—to keep company with God in the ordinary, day-to-day world of eating, working, resting, romancing, aging, earning, grieving, and celebrating."
    —Brian McLaren, author of *A New Kind of Christian*

Available from most booksellers or through Paraclete Press:
www.paracletepress.com; 1-800-451-5006.
Try your local bookstore first.